Introduction to the Musical Brain

by

Don G. Campbell

Introduction to the Musical Brain

by Don G. Campbell

Second Printing 1984
Copyright © 1983 by Magnamusic-Baton, Inc.

ISBN 0-918812 28-3

for Dr. Jean Houston

who is teaching us
to pioneer our unlimited
possibilities

INTRODUCTION TO
THE MUSICAL BRAIN

by

Don G. Campbell

Illustrations by Wanda Bobo

RESERVOIR OF CONTENTS

ACKNOWLEDGEMENTS

Dozens of friends and associates have assisted in making this book a reality:

    Wanda F. Bobo for her drawings and visual suggestions

    Richard S. Orton for his photographs

    Isabel Carley for valuable editing suggestions

    Grace Nash for encouragement and suggestions

    Dr. Robin van Doren Beebe for her left brain clarity for my right brain style

    Ben Zimmerman, M.D.

    Beth Jordan for her proofing

    Dr. Noreen Vickery for her assistance in development

    The students of Dobie Elementary School in Richardson, Texas, for being musical brains

    The students of Cowart Elementary School in Dallas, Texas, for drawing musical brains

    The music teachers in Ft. Myers, Florida, for their willingness to use their kinesthetic senses

    Jenny O'Driscoll, Kate O'Driscoll, Mark Miles, Kathy Johnson, and Ena White for their visual and editorial assistance

    Dudley Lynch of the Brain Technologies Corporation for his helpful seminars

    Almarie Dieckow of Magnamusic-Baton, Inc. who edited the final proof

I am grateful to the following publishers for granting permission to use excerpts from their publications:

The J.T. Tarcher Company of Los Angeles for parts of the exercises from *The Possible Human* by Dr. Jean Houston

Lorin Hollander and Kjos Music Publishers of San Diego for material from Noteworthy Piano News

Jane Prettyman, editor of Dromenon, for the reprinting of "Matters of Consequence" for the appendix

Turnstone Press, Ltd. of Northants, England for permission to quote from Moira Timms' book *The Six o'clock Bus*

Harcourt, Brace and Jovanovich of New York for excerpts from Antoine de St. Exupery's *The Little Prince*

Harper and Row, New York, for permission to quote from Moshe Feldenkrais' *Awareness Through Movement*

Carl Orff/Documentation, His Life and Work. Vol. 3, *The Schulwerk*. Schott Music Corporation, New York, 1978. Translated by Margaret Murray

New Knowledge Books of West Sussex, England for permission to quote from *Music*

Any future response received which concerns other books now out of print will be acknowledged in coming editions or printings.

Above all, my thanks goes to the children of sixty countries at St. Mary's International School in Tokyo, Japan, who introduced me to my musical brain.

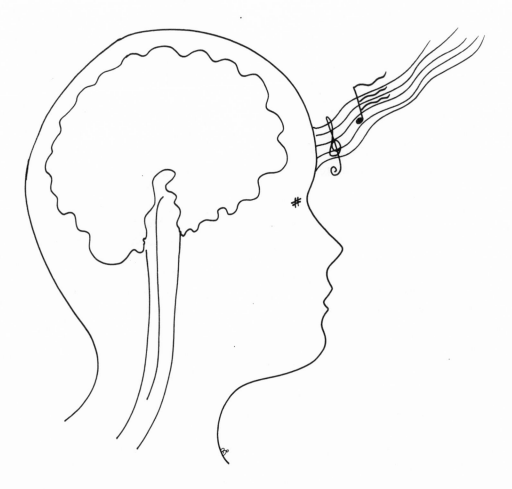

FORETHOUGHTS

At age thirteen I walked into the first classroom of elementary students who would call me teacher. My musical ability was average, my pedagogical skills were purely intuitive and my purpose was to begin my early childhood dream of living with music as much as possible. A clan of small piano students came after school and soon I began to play organ at the church. I loved music, every stitch of it - *West Side Story, The Love for Three Oranges, The Barber of Seville, Moon River,* and anything played on a pipe organ.

At the same time, I was studying with one of the master teachers of all time, Nadia Boulanger. I had been uprooted from a comfortable south Texas community full of choir directors, marching bands, piano recitals, and football games. My whole world quaked with awakening, wonder, and threat. Within a few months my sense of time changed from a centennial Texas to a millennium France. *Easy Steps to Band* was replaced by Hindemith's *Elementary Training for Musicians.* French formality began to co-exist with southern comfort. Music as a gently pressured pleasure became a potent and all-consuming discipline.

Superfluous words had no place in a solfége lesson with Boulanger, yet my own young class, five years younger than I, was not mused by rigor. The quickening of my musical mind did not always integrate with my students' spontaneous play with music. Opposites were at work, using the same elements. Discipline to Boulanger's students meant obsessive work. Discipline to my students meant being quiet and sitting still.

Ten years later I was teaching music to a class of forty first graders in Tokyo. They were from twenty countries and over half did not speak English. My belief that music was an international language was challenged. If music was "in the sighing of a reed and in the gushing of a rill", as Byron tells us, it was not within my trained power to invoke it in those children. Without the English language "preparation for musical experience", teaching could not begin. My college training gave me nothing to lean on because I had no tools to give them verbal instruction. The week that followed changed my outlook on the music process, its meaning and purpose in a student's life. I began to develop an aesthetic plot to involve as much of the child's senses as possible with every lesson and song.

Teaching is as old as humanity. It happens at every stage of social and educational development. Imitation, rote learning, and repetition have never been replaced. Good teaching in our modern context happens because of good planning and well-developed skills. It also happens from spontaneous and unstructured experiences. Great teaching may be a coincidental experience, a focused concentration of "cooperating with the incident."

For twenty years, students have experienced the *AHA!* and *OH NO!* in my classes. Systems such as those in the Waldorf schools and the Summerhill experiments have interested me because of their seemingly higher yield of *AHAs!* Having taught grades one through twelve every day for seven years in a self-contained school, I began to observe how much of the musical technique, information, and enjoyment was retained from one year to the next. I was surprised to find some of the seniors' memories of musical experience coming from lessons in improvisation and experimentation they had received in my junior high classes five years earlier.

Many of the teaching units had been consciously forgotten. I began giving a series of music tests to the upper grades based on units in which they had participated during earlier grades. Hints began to accumulate as to what produced the most significant learning experiences for the whole group. My preparation of the units and my own musical knowledge did not always provide a musical memory. Truly, the most spontaneous, fun, creative, and memorable experiences on their own behalf were the keys, whether the class was of a general classroom nature or a choral setting.

For a thousand years, philosophers and theologians have referred to the head and heart as the two components that give us the genuine status of humanity. Similarly, it has been expressed by the use of the terms mind and feeling, knowledge and understanding, logic and emotion. Always, there has been an attempt to balance these poles. Yet, in Western tradition, the head-knowing logic has developed the structure of our educated societies for both horrid wars and splendid advances in medicine and technology. The feeling and emotional status have always been put in a secondary phase, more passive and less significant. It has represented a feminine aspect in a clichéd form which society is now beginning to change.

The separation of the two functions of the cognitive and affective parts of myself became clear to me in college while reading the analytical handbooks of Dr. Benjamin S.

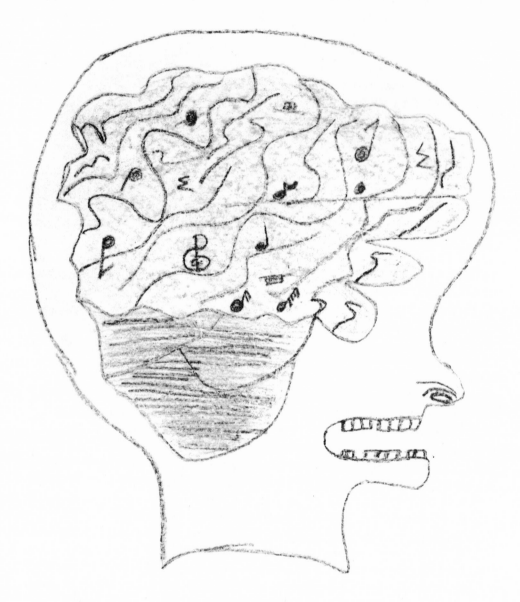

Bloom. His extraordinary point-by-point structured outline, a taxonomy, on the logical and emotional domains of the mind's process impressed me. Often, in teaching, I would return to those outlines to see if my process order followed any of his analytical patterns. Intuitively, I knew there was something of great importance in his logical order, but could not quite come to terms with what it was.

To extend the joy and creative moments of music to others was my goal, but grades, concerts, competitions, and the dread of yearly contests filtered into the picture. Just as children's choirs in churches became obsessed with the Christmas, Easter, and other musical performances of the year, the school became clocked and organized around performing and public programs rather than an inward exploration of the creative mind of the child or youth.

I sought to be more affective, in a logical manner, as well as more sensitive to the expected response of the administration and parents. Slowly, success came in the outer worlds of performance, but I felt that was for the talented twenty percent of the whole student body. What about the others?

The teaching methods and music of Carl Orff have presented more possibilities for my own intuitive path in teaching in a holistic manner. It has granted permission to improvise, visualize, and move within the teaching experience. Many parts of our complex life puzzle began to make a more possible pattern for the *AHA!* to be experienced. By utilizing the Kodaly basics of solfége, my early training with Boulanger became more clearly functional. Eurhythmics came to me by way of the Rudolf Steiner and Emile Jacques-Dalcroze systems. A score of books, gimmicks and well-prepared processes came under my observation and use. My background seemed complete, yet I felt something was missing. There was some link in my teaching that had vanished since I had become a professional. Curiosity prompted me to go to workshops and observe the Alexander Technique of balance, the Feldenkrais Technique of body movement, the Creative Motion Technique for Pianists developed by Margaret Allen, and the Lozanov Method for long range memory in langauges.

Each system had activated an interest in a different part of me. My ability to learn observed itself as partially integrated and largely departmentalized. I taught solfége best in the traditional straight-jacket of a French immovable *"do"* and an immovable body. The choral classroom was still mostly structured around the sit-up-straight, repetitious kneading of repertoire for a performance goal. The Orff classroom was freer and more fun for the younger students than traditional systems. The effectiveness of the church choir rehearsal depended on how many participants would appear for rehearsal and what season it was.

I was not unhappy with the variety of situations because their components were valid and real. But I still felt there were ways to combine the best of the processes so that every student would have a rich and enjoyable experience. I began to transpose one process to another with success. I used Orff methods of improvisation with adult and high school choral ensembles that proved satisfactory, but realized it was slightly awkward for the conditioned, performance oriented singers. I used dance and visualization in solfége class.

Finally, a friend pulled me out of the mainstream of musical possibilities and suggested that I begin reading the basics of gestalt and holistic education. I began a new system of AHA!, connecting the varied sorts of information and processes on which I had depended for many years. Suddenly, I began to realize that the piano student, the dancer, the choral ensemble, the preschool music class and the folk dancer were expressing a similar quest for expression. I remembered a powerful book I had read during my early years in college which had awakened my mind to these creative connections. The book was Robert Henri's The Art Spirit. I began to look back to my own childhood to discern the keys to amusement and discovery that allowed me to dance a discovery, act out a mini-tragedy like a Greek actor, and sing answers to important questions. I held the answers within myself, clutching tightly for fear they would be discarded.

The child and the adult within began to become friends and a process of mental conversations began to join them as advisors and friends. Sometimes the questions were answered in non-verbal forms. There were melodic conversations on teaching points, and all sorts of wild strategies of the metaphoric and symbolic came into play musically and intellectually.

When I first read an article on hemispheric development of the brain in the mid 1970's, I knew that a type of scientific Yin and Yang was being acknowledged by neurologists. As I continued to teach, write and give workshops, I began to observe my own process and the response of the participants. Negative criticism was valuable in creative classes. It usually came from the most authoritarian and intelligent teachers. They were upset because some ideas were not logical; some possibilities were threatening to their own inability to let music move them physically, mentally, kinesthetically and emotionally. Part of me was on their side, saying the more metaphoric manners of musical expression would not stand up in court. But the other part of me was speaking clearly to others, and great encouragement from a few devoted friends allowed me to cross the hurdle of the head and heart syndrome successfully again and again.

The past years have introduced me to the methods and manners of some of the great educators of our time. Jean Houston, George Leonard and Bob Samples stand out as synthesizers of the past, initiating breakthroughs in educational process, personal growth and pioneers of the possible. Their time is ripe and our intuitions should be open, at least, to an awareness of what is both possible and practical.

This book is an introduction to a possibility. It is not a set system of more techniques and processes to add to the caldron of all the other current viewpoints. It aims to enter the general realm of what is happening in brain education and how it can be significant to us as musicians. I am well aware of the danger of generalizations, but I also know the well-documented day of discussion when therapists, neurologists, educators and musicians come to general conclusions is at least a decade away. What is here is a short summary of the general views of the hemispheres, a brief neurological outline of the brain's function and an introduction to some musical experiences which open up the holistic possibilities of music in our overall education.

I write this as a music teacher who has observed his own frustrations and joys in learning. I write in both the singular person of teacher and in the plural of the community of seekers for an integrated approach to art, life and learning. The change in person and in style is purposeful, not to weaken the clarity of meaning, but to add a contrast in thought patterns to the different parts of the reader's brain. I hope a music therapist will write a book which will assist a music teacher in an average classroom. I hope a neurologist will be creative enough to transpose the data of brain research into what Carl Orff knew intuitively about the elemental potency of music. I hope that no reader assumes that I am a writer or a naturally left-brained person.

Above all, I hope that the bridge between heart and mind is strengthened. More confidence in our inner senses will allow us more integration between our logical and emotional potentials. These may be farsighted and idealized goals, but is that not part of an artist's quest in teaching?

Don G. Campbell
Dallas, Texas
March 21, 1983

photo by Richard S. Orton

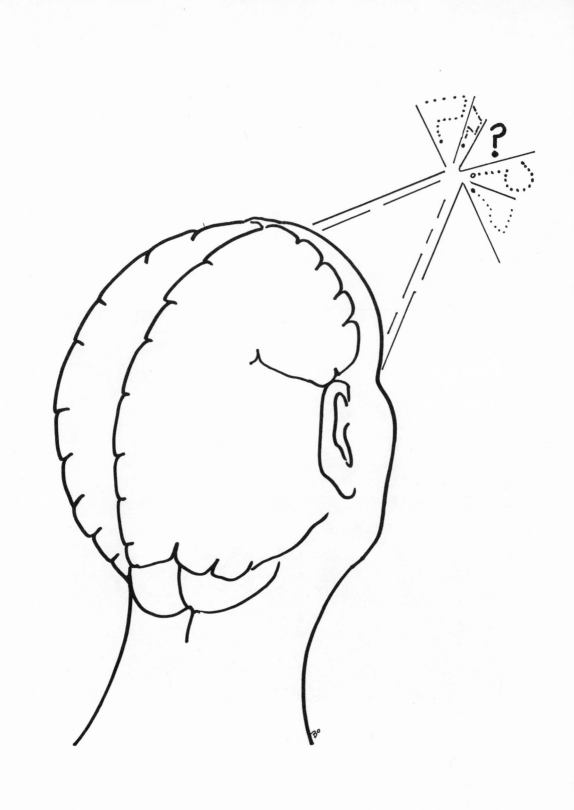

WHERE ARE WE HEADING?

The past twenty years have brought our society to a crossroad of possibility. It is no longer a matter of choosing to continue straight ahead or to turn aside. Our intersections are complexities entangled in a changing educational system, family system and social world. Children are charged with multi-sensory experiences and information. Television has made us aware of a global picture, as near as the next room and as unreal as fantasy and fiction can make it. The wars, the wonders and the commercials are all part of our visual and audio buffet. Yet, we do not assimilate these impressions. We cannot touch them, nor can we smell them. We see them as a person in the fourth tense. Television is a spliced and secondhand view of world trauma mixed with slick cosmetic sales of cars and eyelashes. No longer do grandfathers spend the evenings telling their grandchildren ancient myths and stories. Fairy tales are told by the television and the cinema. The inner images of the princess, the prince, the witch and the dwarfs no longer have time to grow out of the child's imagination. They are packaged and programmed in sight and sound from the child's day of birth.

By the middle part of this century, the idols of Roy Rogers, Sky King and Pinky Lee, Howdy Doody and Superman began to absorb children's play time. Play became more passive, rather than an active part of after-school freedom. Pac-Man and his computer-ized companions are now providing a new trend for children with the rules and stimulation being computerized.

The present models for our children are of a different psychological fabric than the models in previous generations. The children have been charged with stimulation in sight and sound. Yet, we are often using a "Model T" psychology for a diesel child. The basic human components have not changed, but the gear work has been changed. TIME's 1982 Man of the Year was a machine, a computer. Have we lost our sacred archetypes?

In 1978 Bob Samples' book, *The Metaphoric Mind, a Celebration of Creative Consciousness,* came into my hands. It ignited such a series of *AHAs* within me that the fire began to alter my musical process. The crafted words and photographs neither spoke of the music classroom nor of an exact systematized method that would facilitate creative celebration. Yet, the celebration was happening. The reflection, the abstract made a well-defined impression. The book served as a metaphor to music itself.

Metaphor - noun. a figure of speech in which one object is likened to another by speaking of it as if it were that other subject.

Education is heading directly into the metaphor. Our systems have been a chapter in Lewis Carrol's *Alice in Wonderland*, with mad-hattered busing, falling budgets and trial with error strategies for essential learning. Either we must get on with the metaphor of expanding the possibilities of creative learning experiences or we must tighten the seatbelt of the three "R's" and hope the former systems will support future generations. We are truly in the uncomfortable middle, not knowing exactly where to go or what to take with us. It's like being on a jetliner of pioneering potentials with the destination of comprehensive freedom in learning and living.....yet with a flashing "FASTEN SEAT BELT" sign telling us not to move.

We live in a drastic time. Generalizations are dangerous; a little knowledge can prove to be naive and useless. But we must heed the indications on our horizon.

Music teaching has played a significant role in North America in the past thirty years. Probably there is no other area in the world where musical skills have been so greatly exposed to the general public. Marching bands, church choirs and endless types of popular music in recordings and broadcasting have put music in an extraordinary position. Yet, its survival in our educational system is now in question. Thousands of school districts have eliminated music programs in elementary schools. Far more districts have doubled their teachers' duties with less time allowed for each class.

Has music earned a permanent place in the fundamental nature of education or is it still considered an ornament? **The question of music as a part of leisure, pleasure and entertainment versus its power as an enabling agent for human learning at large is now at hand.** Are we going to be able to keep the public and financially-ruling boards interested in music by presenting a few concerts per year and an enjoyable class where students have the attitude of non-learning?

I do not wish to imply that great teaching is not taking place. It is! The apparent result of musical interest and learning is to be seen and heard. The question is: how effective will we be as musicians and educators in retaining our positions if funds are not supplied?

4

I detest fear tactics and Doomesbury's theories (pun intended) which threaten us into social molds. But I do realize there are facts which should be observed in view of our future educational conditions.

> If the world were a global village of 100 people, 70 of them would be unable to read, and only one would have a college education. Over 59 would be suffering from malnutrition and over 80 would live in what we call substandard housing. If the world were a global village of 100 residents, 6 of them would be Americans. These six would have half the village's income and the other 94 would exist on the other half. How would the "wealthy 6" live in peace with their neighbors?
>
> from *The Six O'Clock Bus* by Moira Timms

These are disturbing facts. The point of this book on the musical brain perhaps seems a universe away from the world-globe reality. There is a connection and one that possibly points us to the next century. That is, facing the music of the human, its dire and important function in all cultures, with its common denominator of communication in the expressive and non-verbal worlds, to logical and grammatical society. Elemental music communicates. The globe and our communities are not generally interested in Bartok's string quartets, Bach's motets or Indian ragas. These are often esoteric languages to society. But the musical elements of simple feelings, emotional reflection, dominating marches and pulsating dances bring a large group of people to united attention.

It is believed that the elemental response to music falls into the lower parts of the brain and the right brain. The development of musical forms, sophisticated analysis and harmonic understanding lie in the left hemisphere. It is too simple to say we have two brains. We may have three, five, ten or ten billion. The following chapters spell out these generalities in a more specific manner.

The question as to where we are heading implies the awareness of our musicianship, its base and elemental being, as well as its educated and sophisticated scope. We should not put our performance values in jeopardy, nor our education in a drawer. It is necessary, however, to consider the parts of music which are elemental to our humanity and judge if we are still feeding our natural, rhythmic being, which is far older than has been thought.

Orff, Kodaly, Steiner, Suzuki and other prominent educators looked at the importance of the music process earlier in the century before the television and audio tape were influential. They made some essential statements about the philosophy and purpose of music.

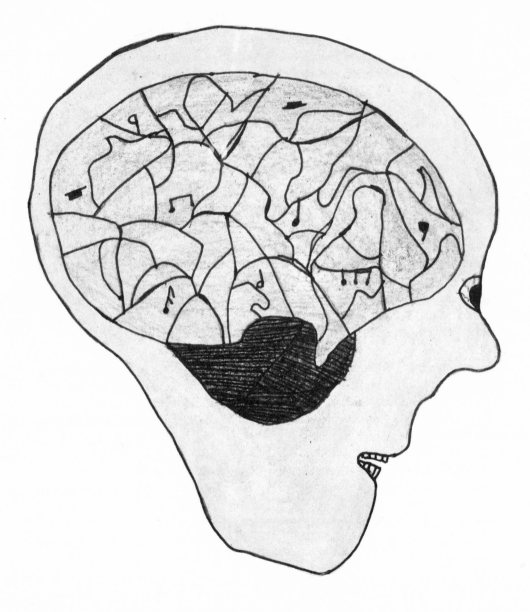

Rudolf Steiner:

> If one seeks a true knowledge of man, one should study the human form not only as it presents itself to the eye, from an anatomical point of view, but one should try to add an inner *musical* understanding for the forces which brought about this form. If one is able to achieve such an inner understanding of the creative musical forces, then one will discover that music can be *seen* everywhere in the world. It is there, if only one can find it.[1]

Carl Orff:

> Because I do not wish to speak technically about all the questions of educational reform that are being discussed so much in all parts of the world today, I should like to express my thoughts in an untechnical way that should be easy to understand. For this we must return again to nature. Elementary music, word and movement, play, everything that awakens and develops the powers of the spirit, this is the 'humus' of the spirit, the humus without which we face the danger of a spiritual erosion. When does erosion occur in nature? When the land is wrongly exploited; for instance when the natural water supply is disturbed through too much cultivation, or when, for utilitarian reasons, forests and hedges fall as victims of drawing-board mentality; in short, when the balance of nature is lost by interference. In the same way I would like to repeat: Man exposes himself to spiritual erosion if he estranges himself from his elementary essentials and thus loses his balance.
>
> Just as humus in nature makes growth possible, so elementary music gives to the child powers that cannot otherwise come to fruition. It is at the primary school age that the imagination must be stimulated; and opportunities for emotional development, which contain experience of the ability to feel, and the power to control the expression of that feeling, must also be provided. Everything that a child of this age experiences, everything in him that has been awakened and nurtured is a determining factor for the whole of his life. Much can be destroyed at this age that can never be regained, much can remain undeveloped than can never be reclaimed.[2]

[1] from *Music*, edited by Lionel Stebbing, New Knowledge Books, West Sussex.

[2] Carl Orff/Documentation, His Life and Work. Vol. 3, *The Schulwerk*. Schott Music Corporation, New York, 1978. Translated by Margaret Murray.

Shinichi Suzuki:

> Let us think of how talent is cultivated. I like to use the phrase "capacity of brain" to mean the capacity to achieve talent and use it. To discover the "capacity of the brain" is one point we have yet to solve in all the problems we have in regard to education. Scholars of heredity may say that the talents for music, mathematics or literature are there when the baby is born, but I wish to disagree on this point. My reason is that the matter of heredity is within the limit of psychological conditions, whereas culture, built up by mankind, cannot be passed on physically.

> I wish to define the meaning of the phrase "brain capacity" to mean the ability to catch one's surroundings and to realize it. In other words, to take in things outside of oneself and to work it into a sort of energy within one's self and bring it out by actions.
>   — from an address given to the MENC National Convention, Philadelphia, 1964.

Zoltan Kodaly:

> Music education contributes to the many-sided capabilities of a child, affecting not only specifically musical aptitudes but his general hearing, his ability to concentrate, his conditional reflexes, his emotional horizon and his physical culture.
>   — from a lecture

Emile Jacques-Dalcroze:

> The aim of eurhythmics is to enable pupils, at the end of their course, to say, not "I know," but "I have experienced," and so to create in them the desire to express themselves; for the deep impression of an emotion inspires a longing to communicate it, to the extent of one's powers, to others. The more we have of life, the more we are able to diffuse life about us. "Receive and give!" is the golden rule of humanity; and if the whole system of rhythmic training is based on music, it is because music is a tremendous psychic force: a product of our creative and expressive functions that, by its power of stimulating and disciplining, is able to regulate all our vital functions.

> The education of the nervous system must be of such a nature that the suggested rhythms of a work of art induce in the individual analogous vibrations, produce a powerful reaction in him and change naturally into rhythms of expression. In simpler language, the body must become capable of responding to artistic rhythms and of realizing them quite naturally without fear of exaggeration.
>   — from early writings and lectures

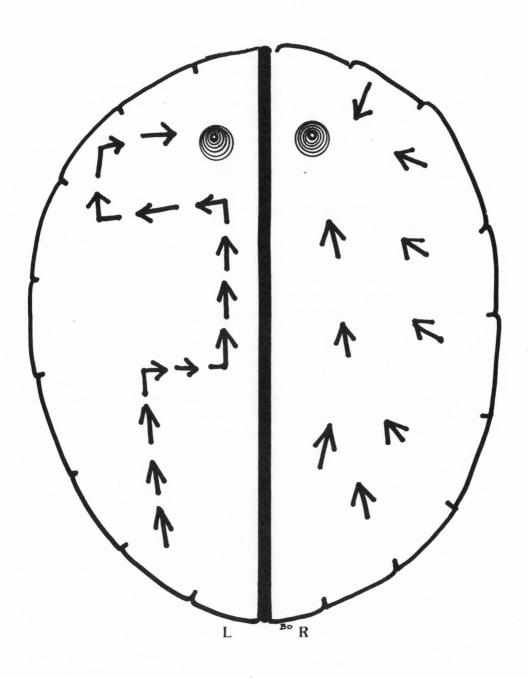

L   BO R

Common generalizations of the left and right hemispheres of the neo-cortex are shown by the process the arrows follow to realize an idea. This simplification is an example of the right brain's mode of visual symbolism.

Music therapists have been devoted to the powers of music within specialized classrooms and learning environments. Gertrude Orff extended her husband's work through an exceptional book on the subject, *The Orff Music Therapy*. The brain research of the past years has also been very specialized, with data coming from people who have needed to have their brain hemispheres separated due to illness or cases of epilepsy. The statistics are interesting, yet the testing was done with abnormal brain conditions. The transposition of this information has not yet been successfully communicated to the general classroom and choral teacher for any practical use.

Our libraries are growing rapidly with information of interest for musicians. Our record collections enable us to hear more music in a year than people could have heard in a lifetime a century ago. Our educated circuits are moving so rapidly that it is a full-time task to keep up with periodicals, texts and professional reports in our area of study. To add to a full-time teacher's duties is nearly impossible. A couple of workshops per year and a summer at a nearby university every few years is perhaps all the updating of data and discovering of new materials that is possible.

Flags are being raised in our own communities without any awareness of global identity. Music teachers have crowded classrooms, children who cannot read, small budgets for instruments or recordings, and are faced with having to be retrained for certification in another subject. Our heads should be concerned for ourselves and our own children. We have an investment in our education and lifetime earning possibilities. The children will determine if the arts are to be patronized in the future. We are part of that history. The time is exciting, the time is demanding, the time is complex and the time to put our heads together is NOW.

WE MUST RETURN THE ARTS TO THE SCHOOLS. IN THE ARTS, THE WHOLE PROCESS IS DONE FROM BEGINNING TO END. SO OFTEN, WE LEAVE OUT THE MIDDLE IN EDUCATION.

— Dr. Jean Houston

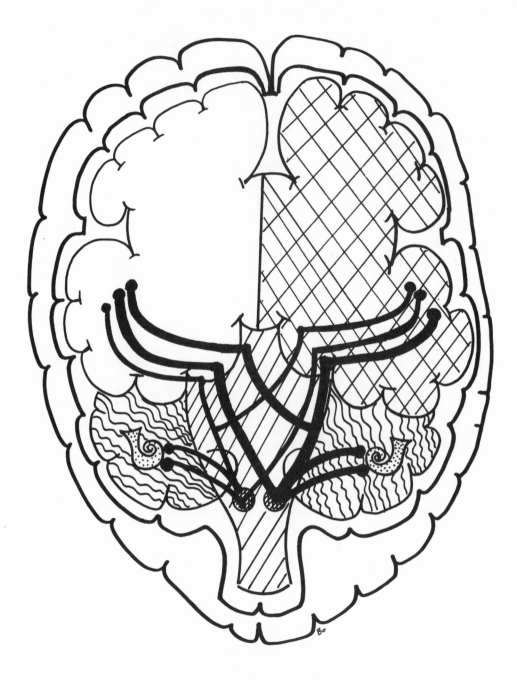

THE BRAIN BOWL

Philosophers and scientists have been theorizing on the functions and nature of the brain since the time when Hippocrates located the center of thought within the head. The scope of variation in memory, creative potential and automatic controls within the brain produces a counterpoint of chemical and electrical activity that is as extensive as a galaxy. The brain and mind can be viewed from so many standpoints that generalizations are nearly impossible. From the cave of Plato to the holographic theories of Pribram, speculation has provided hundreds of maps for understanding the brain's process.

Musicians find the scientific data of interest when it is relevant to the way music is perceived and processed. The wide variety of neurological data and medical observations cannot ususally be translated into practical suggestions for better teaching or learning. The mammoth maze of the brain is too complex and complicated for the finest minds in the field to generalize. It is therefore necessary for the musical investigation of the brain to be introduced simply in terms of what is known to be relevant to the learning and the teaching of music.

If the brain were a map of the United States, knowledge of its highways would exist from New York City to Princeton, New Jersey. The goal to travel to San Diego is known and there are strong suggestions as to what the landscape would be in the territory between Princeton and San Diego. But the exact mapping is yet to done. Brain research has just begun to see where the highways are within the skull. The diversity of research and statistics provide many clues which have yet to come to a full view as to how the brain learns, remembers and functions.

The most significant point that can be made to musicians and artists who have interest in the brain studies is:

THE MORE CONNECTIONS THAT CAN BE MADE IN THE BRAIN, THE MORE INTEGRATED THE EXPERIENCE IS WITHIN MEMORY.

That statement is the premise of this book. What does it mean? It means that through the understanding of the workings of:

> A. The nervous system and the parts of the brain
> B. The Triune Brain Theory
> C. Right Brain and Left Brain Theories
> D. The Holographic Brain Theory

that existing methods of teaching and experiencing music can be enhanced. This also implies that music can be used to increase memory and perception in other fields of study.

A. THE NERVOUS SYSTEM AND THE PARTS OF THE BRAIN

By making two fists, the brain can be represented. It is a divided, walnut-shaped maze of nearly 12 billion cells. It weighs slightly over three pounds and looks like an undefined series of lumps and lines of pinkish gray matter with the texture of soft, unprocessed cheese. Millions of pieces of information are mysteriously stored in this small area. Here the autonomic parts of our body functions are regulated and unconsciously organized. Thousands of chemical and electrical actions take place within the smallest measurable fraction of a second. The brain's multi-dimensional jigsaw of function and information fits and interplays within itself, creating dreams onto a nocturnal video screen, unique aspects of behaviour and personality, and the endless variety of learning, responding, parenting and feeling which constitute our unique human nature.

In the adult brain, there are more than 10,000,000,000 or 10 to the ninth power nerve cells. Most of these are comparable to a small computer which is programmed through a combination of chemicals and electricity. Most of them are formed by the end of the first year of life. Since they do not divide like other cells, they cannot replace themselves. It is curious that nearly 10,000 of these neurons die each day beyond the age of 21 so that the weight of the brain decreases with age. That, however, does not seem to be the important factor in loss of memory. The connection of as many neurons as possible within a learning experience increases the capacity of long range memory. By learning how to "program" as many of these neurons as possible, our musical experiences will have points of reference. Most neurons can link up with 200,000 others, but the average one usually connects with 60,000. A quadrillion connections are possible.

Each neuron has three parts: the cell body, the axon and the dendrites. These are distantly comparable to the trunk, roots and branches of a tree. Through the chemical and electrical charges caused by a combination of sodium and potassium, the neurons send signals to one another. This signal jumps from the positive axon to the receptive dendrite. Each neuron seems to send exactly the same type of signal on an electrical level with a variance in its frequency depending on the intensity of the experience.

The Receiving Dendrites

The Sending Axon

THE NEURON

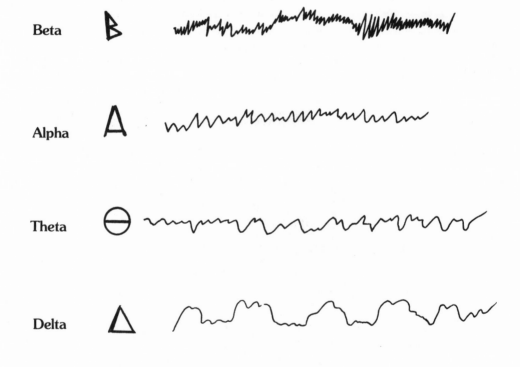

Beta

Alpha

Theta

Delta

The Wave Forms of the Brain

When this electrical signal leaves a neuron, it passes through an axon. It fires a chemical called a neurotransmitter across a gap, called a synapse, to the receptive dentrite of another neuron. That triggers another electrical signal in its neighboring neuron, which in turn, produces another neurotransmitter.

Millions of neurons can be activated in a single experience. Music has an uncanny manner of activating neurons for purposes of relaxing muscle tension, changing pulse and producing long-range memories which are directly related to the number of neurons activated in the experience. This can now be measured by injecting the brain with radioactive chemicals that are detected when the brain cells are active.

The speed of the electrical activity of the brain is measured in four wave forms. The *Beta* wave is the most common type of activity found in our normal, conscious states. These waves undulate from 18 to 40 cycles per second. This activity is mostly recorded in the frontal and parietal regions of the cortex.

Alpha waves are commonly found when one is quiet and resting. Music can induce this state and can activate a kind of creative daydreaming. Usually the eyes are closed and there is no type of problem solving taking place. The Alpha waves are formed in the frequency range of 8 to 12 cycles per second.

Theta waves are observed mainly in the temporal and pariental regions of children's brains and occasionally in adults experiencing great stress from disappointment or frustration. They can also be observed in states of high creativity. These waves are formed between 4 and 7 cycles per second.

Delta waves are found in very deep states of sleep with the waves forming every 1 to 3 cycles per second. Breathing is deep, the blood pressure decreases as well as the heartbeat and body temperature. This state is unconscious and the least understood. It is not likely to occur in a music class!

All of the information that follows concerns itself with the construction of the different parts of the brain. The musician should keep in mind that the stimulation of more neurons produces greater memory. The different parts of the brain and the nervous system filter and process information in different ways which are relevant to the musical mind and overall memory. These different ways provide us with some clues which assist in our listening and teaching processes.

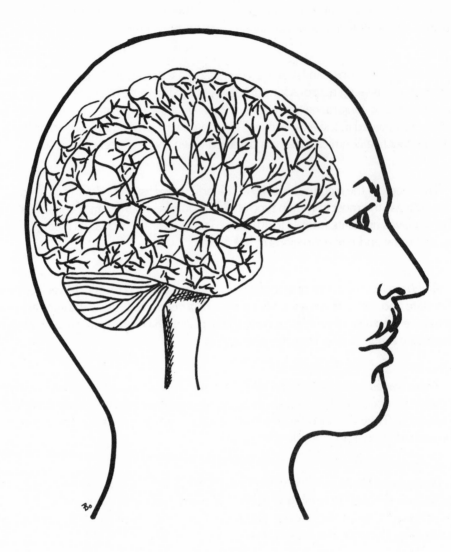

The Blood Vessels of the Brain

The brain cells are kept alive and functioning by oxygen, which is brought to the brain by blood. While the brain makes up approximately two percent of the body's weight, it consumes from 19% to 25% of the body's oxygen. In all other parts of the body, the measurement of blood-oxygen is directly proportionate to the amount of physical work done. The brain receives twenty percent of all the blood that is pumped from the heart and regulates its own flow. The more blood and oxygen in the brain seems to increase intellectual activity. Any class, whether it is music or not, is likely to yield a higher rate of retention if the blood flow to the brain is not inhibited.

The brain is both a sending and a receiving agent of the nervous system. The transmission of thought to physical action passes through hundreds of networks, jumping the spaces between the neurons and relaying messages simultaneously from the eyes and ears at varying speeds. Depending on the familiarity of the action, the sending and response to these messages can travel from three to over two hundred miles an hour.

Consider an organist sitting at a keyboard, preparing to play a Bach fugue. The body automatically sits in a playing position. The registration for the volume and tone color is selected and attention is given visually to the printed score. As the organist begins to play, information is directed from the neo-cortex, the frontal portions of the brain, through the middle brain and lower portions, then to the brainstem and a complex mixmaster of nerve centers in the shoulder, where the command for each of the fingers is properly sorted out. The information then enters the radial, media and ulnar nerves in the arms and hands.

The relay of physical motion, emotional sensations and sensory awareness of sound and touch are integrated with reading skills, performance interpretation and memory of previous musical experiences in the organist. Different portions of the brain process the experience simultaneously. The lowest portions of the brain take care of the physical systems of the body. The brainstem serves as the cable which carries the information to the rest of the body. The largest part of this lower brain is the cerebellum which is the co-ordinating area for muscle movement. It works on an autonomic and subconscious level to keep the higher portions of the brain informed of the motion of the fingers, feet, arms and legs. It balances and controls the organist's wrists, hands and leg muscles for smooth and properly executed playing. The cerebellum looks like two small pear-shaped lobes with horizontal creases around the outside portion.

Above this area is an important area for musical processing. The limbic system consists of a number of areas with specific tasks:

The Limbic System

The hypothalamus regulates the temperature of the body, the desire for food and is part of the pain, depression and pleasure responses. *(The organist has no physical demands which detract from playing.)*

The hippocampus develops short-term memory and prepares messages for other parts of the brain to store information permanently. *(The organist prepares minor details for playing.)*

The basal ganglia regulates balance and the movement of the body. *(The organist balances on the bench and places the hands and feet in comfortable positions.)*

The amygdala is a processing place for old memories and habits as they travel to the cortex. *(The organist has some fear and anxiety, perhaps stage fright, because of past experiences in performance.)*

The thalamus receives information from the senses and relays the information to different areas of the cortex. *(The organist sees the music, plays the keys and hears the sound.)*

The limbic system is essential in the emotional processing of a musician. Both learning and motivative behavior are seated here. Often, classifications are made to the right and left hemispheres of the brain which belong in the limbic system. This system has no words, no self-evaluation or criticism. It is deeper, stronger and more elemental to our basic nature than the opinions expressed by the higher parts of the brain. The urge to make music, to dance and to imitate movement are seated in the limbic system.

The cortex is the covering of the brain and is the large area that controls our intelligence and higher mental activities. This cerebral area is most developed in dolphins and humans. Here sensations, experienced and registered as voluntary actions, are initiated. It has been called the seat of our humanity because of its ability to store facts as memory. Here, we make decisions and formulate logic. The organist is using this area to read music by interpreting the symbols that have been previously studied. The act of playing comes to realization and the music is stylized and experienced. Memorization takes place in the cortex as does the remembrance of melodies and other musical experiences.

The cortex is divided into two lobes or hemispheres, each with its own tendencies of the kind of information it processes. These two lobes are connected by hundreds of thousands of small fibers called the *corpus callosum*. Most of the popular attention given to the brain in recent years has emphasized these two lobes by calling them the left and right brains. This classification has allowed the teacher and the learner to understand a variety of mental processes. Yet, there are more portions of this cerebral cortex than just the generalized right and left lobes. Within the cortex is also found:

The parietal lobe selects which information coming into the brain will be attended and handled. It receives information which can interpret special details and the sense of touch. *(The organist realizes a difficult passage for fingering is approaching.)*

The temporal lobe is the center for hearing and memory of information communicated through sound. *(The organist compares what is being played and what has been played at other times.)*

The frontal lobe or neo-cortex is the newest and most highly developed part of the brain. It can process the future, plan in advance and relate altruism, as well as holistic goals. *(The organist senses the music of the spheres as an empowering agent to help humanity.)*

The brain is so complex and interconnected that it is difficult to separate its functions and areas into simple generalizations. The musician may not know what is happening in the brain and think it is of no importance to the performance of a composition. It cannot be assumed that such information will automatically assist in the improvement of musical performance. There are, however, parts of the cortex that send and receive information which can alter both learning and performing experiences.

The cortex has an area around the top of the head which extends toward the top of the ears and which responds to the sensory functions of the body. This area is called the sensory *homonculus* meaning *little man*. It receives the impressions of touch, physical motion and the majority of motor skills. The sensory area on the right part of the brain receives information from the left side of the body as the sensory area on the left part of the cortex receives information from the right side of the body. The amount of area of the cortex devoted to the different parts of the sensory detectors in the body is determined by their use. There are large areas in this section of the brain which are activated by the mouth, lips and fingers.

The motor homunculus runs parallel to the sensory homunculus. It is the sending station for the physical activities of the body. It controls the physical movements on the opposite side of the body. Large areas are given to the thumbs, fingers, hands and head.

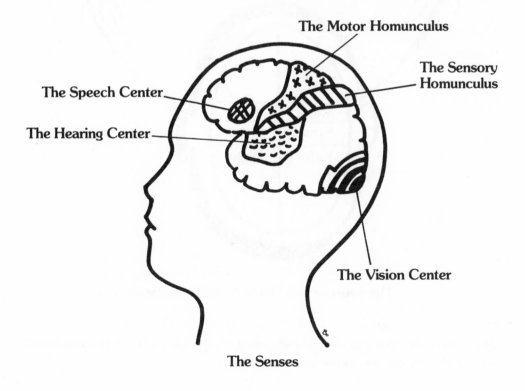

The Senses

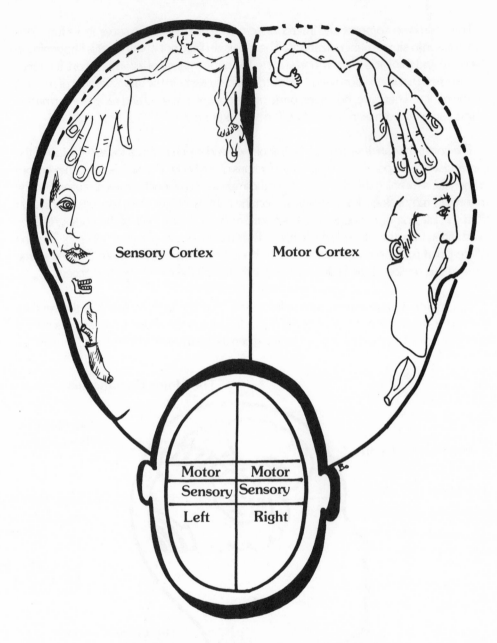

The Sensory and Motor Areas of the Brain

The parts of the body that are most sensitized are represented by these proportional areas in the sensory and motor areas of the brain.

These two areas are important to the organist because the knowledge and experience of listening and playing come to consciousness. These areas are important in the learning process. When they are stimulated, the brain is awakened to more potential. Multisensory integration can take place in these areas and the musician, the athlete and the artist can magnify learning through their activation.

THE MORE CONNECTIONS THAT CAN BE MADE IN THE BRAIN, THE MORE INTEGRATED THE EXPERIENCE IS WITHIN MEMORY.

The exercises in the last portion of this book focus on the use of multisensory experiences for learning by activating the motor and sensory areas of the cortex.

Educators have assumed that the majority of musical attention and aptitude takes place within the auditory system. This is so obvious that the rest of the brain and body has often been neglected as being agents of musical experiences. As the two dimensions of auditory stimuli, amplitude and frequency, interact, sounds are produced. Distortion of small hair-like cilia in the receptor areas of the inner ear evoke neural impulses. These microscopic cilia grow and seemingly float on a membrane within the cochlea. Their ends float in the cochlear fluid, reaching out to invite excitation from any vibrations transmitted there from the middle-ear chamber. These cilia are very similar to the ones in the semicircular canals where balance and movement are assessed. Here, any movement in the head causes an inertial counter-movement in the fluid, bringing excitation to the cilia.

Loudness is determined by the number of cilia brought to excitation. Here, sound information is changed from physical stimulus (movement) to electrochemical charges in the neurons comprizing the membrane. We must consider that the individual neurons working with each other in concert is humongous. That these electro-chemical reports are sent to multi-layered areas of the brain, spreading from each axon to thousands of dendrites in the next layer and so on and so forth, the complexity of our comprehending system quickly moves out of reason. It is so immense that it is unbelievable we can hear anything but cacaphony when a pin drops or a thunderous dissonance when an oboe plays.

Most of the auditory impulses cross over into the opposite lobe of the brain from the ear hearing the sound. The frequency of pitches, as well as the tonal color, seem to localize in different parts of the cortex. Some pitches stay on the same side of the brain as the ear that is hearing a sound. The inner ear is made up of a spiraled chamber called the cochlea. It is here that the tiny hairs are activated. The ones on the inner spiral respond to lower frequencies and the ones on the outer spiral respond to higher frequencies.

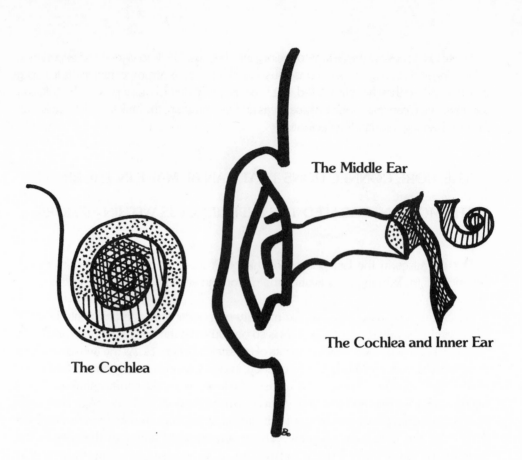

The Middle Ear

The Cochlea and Inner Ear

The Cochlea

The Auditory System

The complexity of the brain and its functions may not interest musicians beyond the information given in this chapter, but an awareness of some of its basic duties can activate a more thorough approach to teaching. In the following sections, three major theories of brain research are explained for the purpose of assisting the musician's outlook in teaching and learning.

B. THE TRIUNE BRAIN THEORY

Dr. Paul MacLean, Chief of the Laboratory of Brain Evolution and Behavior at the National Institute of Mental Health in Washington, D.C., has developed a theory over the past thirty years which divides the systems of the brain into three parts which mirror behavior in reptiles and mammals. He points out quite clearly that the human has three brains, two of which are similar to those found in lower forms of life. His research was stimulated by his background in medical school at Harvard and his father, a minister. During his army career, he became aware of human cooperation and empathy to a greater degree than in the academic world. This triggered his investigation of how the brain works with ideals and moral concepts.

He summarizes his theory in the Fall, 1980, issue of <u>Dromenon.</u>

> In its development, the human forebrain has expanded to a great size, while retaining the basic features of three formations that reflect our relationship to reptiles, early mammals and recent mammals. Radically different in structure and chemistry, and, in an evolutionary sense, countless generations apart, the three formations constitute a hierarchy of three brains in one, or what may be called for short, a **triune** brain. Such a situation indicates that we are obliged to look at ourselves and the world through the eyes of three quite different mentalities. As a further complication, there is evidence that the two older mentalities lack the necessary neural machinery for verbal communication. But to say that they lack the power of speech does not belittle their intelligence, nor does it relegate them to a realm of the "unconscious." Educationally, these are significant considerations, because it is usually assumed that we are dealing with a single intelligence. How much weight should we give to intelligence tests that largely ignore two of our ever-present personalities because they cannot read or write?

The first brain that MacLean recognizes is the lowest area, just above the brainstem. This "reptilian" brain is not different from that in turtles, lizards, crocodiles and their kin. As the bottom core of our present brain, it is concerned with physical space, basic survival, possessions, and the urges of self-defense. The biological and physical functions of the body are co-ordinated from this area. When a musician is missing a music stand or is forced to sit in a section of an orchestra that is different from a standard place, this reptilian brain reacts. Rituals of tuning and dress also establish part of a musician's natural mannerisms stemming from this brain.

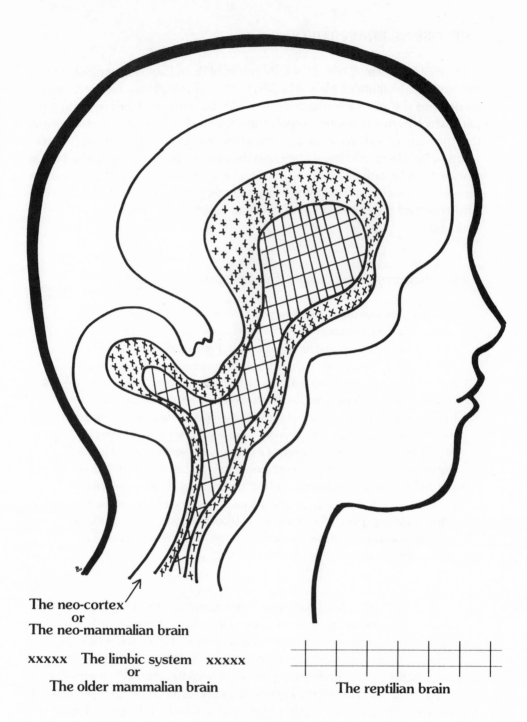

The neo-cortex
or
The neo-mammalian brain

xxxxx   The limbic system   xxxxx
or
The older mammalian brain

The reptilian brain

The Triune Brain

The middle brain or the "mammalian" brain is composed of the limbic system. This brain is similarly found in horses, rabbits and rats. The limbic system is involved with the processing of emotions. The social and family sense of concern and protection is seated in this area. Strong convictions arise from this area especially in religious and political views. No matter what is true or false, the strength of opinion overrules the higher aspects of logic. Here the musician resides in a defined musical family.

When new forms of music enter the repertoire or a more talented musician challenges another musician's position, the limbic system is likely to react. Here resides the emotional basis of music which speaks to universal groups. Perhaps this is the place of origin of what Carl Orff meant by "Elemental Music".

The neo-cortex is the third part of MacLean's brain map. It is intellectual and conceptual. It responds to ideas and creates new modes of thinking in the sciences, arts, and religion. This neo-cortex is called the neo-mammalian brain. Reading, writing, logic, mathematics, abstract thought and logical processes all exist within the two lobes of this frontal area of the brain. Religious music and pure motives of human ethics, such as expressed in Beethoven's Ninth Symphony, exist here.

There is a "community of learning" within these three brains. Teamwork, cooperation, independent research, emotional response, physical comfort and satisfaction, are all important to musical experiences. Music can activate, stimulate or disrupt the flow of the processes taking place in the limbic system. This is deeper and more potent than musical opinions which take place in the cortex. Social and academic structures usually wish to leave the primitive and keenly emotional parts of being in the hind areas of social appearance. Rather than incorporate them into a directed holistic function, they are usually tied to conditioned habits and social mores. Children for the past fifty years have been asked to sit still, listen and recite their factual knowledge by rote. MacLean believes that the incorporation of these three areas will awaken a fuller and more satisfying manner of learning.

Fifteen years ago, a progressive and pioneering woman, Dr. Elaine de Beauport, started the Mead School in Byram, Connecticut. In its development, she sought to increase the role of the less dominant parts of the brain in education. (See Appendix I for a detailed interview with Dr. de Beauport) She utilized art, music, crafts and poetry in her classes and found reading, science and math achievement improved. In a recent interview, she stated,

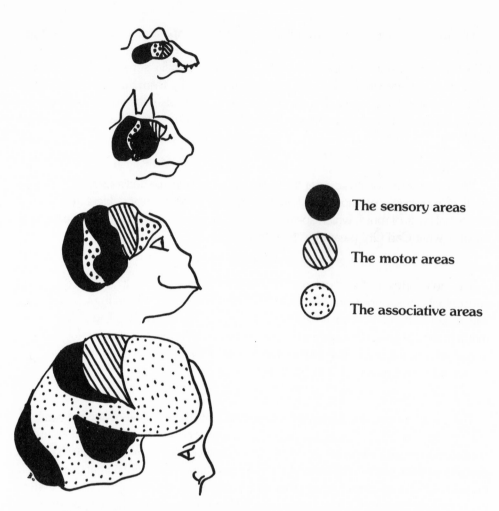

The sensory areas

The motor areas

The associative areas

The triune brain provides a model for kids to know themselves and for teachers to be sure they're leaving nothing out. It gives us a whole new charter for education: a general systems approach to the workings of the human mind. We no longer have to think of ourselves as separate from other forms of life. What's missing from our educational efforts? The *feeling* brain. Affection was the first characteristic of mammalian growth. It's important to remember that half of our bodies are controlled by feelings. It's not the doctor who should be taking care of the ulcer when you're fifty, it's the educational process that should take care of it when you're five.

The musical implications of the triune brain have far-reaching possibilities in assisting children to improve their reading, writing and mathematic skills. This area may well provide the new manners of music teaching that will ensure a place for arts in the curriculum.

C. RIGHT BRAIN/LEFT BRAIN THEORIES

Most of the articles and publicity given to brain research in the past few years have been in the area of Left Brain/Right Brain studies. Many of the popular summaries of the work assume that opposites exist in the frontal lobes of the cerebral cortex. This is a vague and a greatly challenged subject. Research has verified that the two hemispheres do process information in different manners. It has also been proven that each side of the brain has the capacity for being encoded with the ability to operate for both sides of the brain.

In 1981, three Nobel Prizes were awarded to doctors who had done remarkable work on the divided functions of the hemispheres of the cortex. Dr. Roger Sperry's research was done in the 1960's and 1970's on the disparate function of the lobes. That work has influenced most other studies in the field. He studied patients whose nerve endings had been separated as a necessity for their health. He found that when the connections between the cortical lobes were severed, they were totally oblivious to each other. The corpus callosum that connects the two lobes is essential for normal adults. Because the treatment and observation in this research was done with mostly epileptic patients, it is difficult to translate the data into normal learning circumstances. It was learned, however, that when the separation occurred, truly the right hand did not know what the left hand was doing. In his classic experiments, Sperry showed different symbols to each eye of patients with separated lobes. For instance, he let a patient see a dollar sign with the left eye and a question mark with the right eye. Generally, the left hand and eye are controlled with the right side of the brain. The results proved that two independent streams of consciousness exist within the brain which can be cut off entirely from each other.

This research generally upset the conventional belief that the left hemisphere is superior. Sperry's research states that the right hemisphere "is clearly superior to the left in many respects especially regarding the capacity for concrete thinking, spatial consciousness and comprehension of complex relationships." The right lobe is also superior in interpreting auditory impressions and distinguishing voices, intonations and musical experiences.

Outgrowth of this research has found tendencies for the brains of younger boys and girls to be localized differently. Female infants were more sensitive to sounds, voices and noises than boys. Boys tended to be more clumsy in fine motor tuning, but overall, more controlled in total body co-ordination. Female infants also speak sooner, possess a greater vocabulary and are less apt to show speech problems, such as stuttering. Testing is now being done with young children and their response to music, motor tuning and speech problems. Although the data is still inconclusive,

31

it is apparent that by use of music as 'a method to integrate the body and speech movements, results are more quickly observed.[3]

Why there is localization of certain abilities, processes and responses is an arena of scientific speculation. The following two chapters discuss in more detail the classifications and generalization of the left and right lobes in regard to a musician's education.

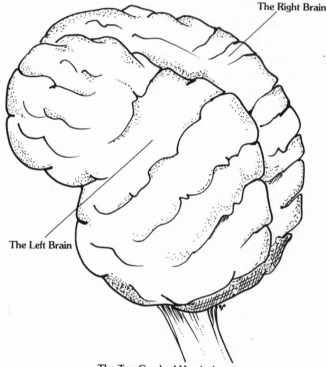

The Right Brain

The Left Brain

The Two Cerebral Hemispheres

[3] The most complete series of studies in the neurological aspects of music has been compiled in a detailed book of twenty-five essays edited by MacDonald Critchley and R.A. Henson in England. *Music and the Brain, Studies in the Neurology of Music* is published by William Heinemann Medical Board. The detailed studies are of academic interest, yet give few clues for practical application. The data, however, is essential to therapists and those wishing to pursue this study from a medical standpoint.

D. THE HOLOGRAPHIC BRAIN THEORY

One of the most interesting theories of brain function deals with the brain as a singular unit rather than a split or triunal division. Karl Pribram of Stanford University has provided a holographic model of the brain in his research on memory. In his early career as a neurosurgeon he believed there was not enough data to justify the widespread use of lobotomies. One of his major discoveries was the relationship between the frontal lobes and the limbic system. His experiments proved that monkeys without their frontal lobes could still be assertive at times. From those experiments, he later challenged the basic function of brain cells, by declaring they were part of an elegant feedback circuit rather than a simple reflex. From that point, he began to believe that the brain operated on mathemathical principles similar to that of a hologram. This theory explains that *similar* bits of memory information are stored in different parts of the brain. Although his initial theory was regarded as being metaphoric, there is now adequate evidence that his model has a physiological basis. It is similar to Aristotle's theory that the ideal form dominates mental life on every level, from the natural biological order to the social order. In other words, the whole can be constructed from any part.

Pribram entertains the possibility that memory storage works like a hologram. Bits of information are stored ubiquitously throughout the brain. Each neuron would have the capacity and efficiency to store billions of these bits. This information resonates like a bell and the waves encode other neurons with the same pitches and overtones. There are instances when people have had strokes and, with only two percent of the fibers remaining in working order, have returned to near normal mental function. Memory would therefore be distributed in every part of the brain, localized in no particular section. Pribram maintains that both the brain tissue and holograms can be cut up without destroying the capacity to process and remember images. We cannot help speculating how memory, in this theory, would affect us musically. It is as if every tone is held within a single tone. This implies that all sounds are held within the overtones and harmonics of each fundamental pitch. This is partially true, especially if Hans Kayser's important work *Akroasis, The Theory of World Harmonics,* is regarded as a musical holograph. Some of the speculations of Pythagoras, Kepler and Fludd seem to have introduced these ideas in their view of the music of the spheres.

To be able to grasp the dimension of a visual hologram is difficult to explain without seeing it. The verbal and logical translation of what is happening in a hologram does not awaken the dynamic sensory impressions of an actual viewing, of a three-dimensional sculpture in mid-air consisting of light. To translate a similar model to brain theory in a simplified manner is also difficult to explain.

Pribram calls the distribution of memory a *hololologic representation* because it is not necessarily dependent on the visual or graphic, point-to-point representation. By awakening a small segment of a memory, a cue for total recall is established. Partial re-enactment of neural activity can release specific recollection of full sensory experiences of an event.

Most of the logical memory systems classify information. One must know some kind of classification system to find information in books, tapes, films and recordings. Libraries are classified by indexes and by an order of shelving the books. The computer works in a similar manner, yet the brain does not seem to be quite so systematized. In the hololologic system, a hint of a few words or melodic bits would instantly recall all its associations.

This hololologic mode of processing and storage comes closer to a sympathetic vibration than other theories. As research develops, the musician may come to realize the power of music to activate greater segments of memory.

Hugo Zuccarelli, an Italian living in London, has made an extraordinary advance in brain research by creating a method of broadcasting sound to the brain without the use of normal acoustical channels. Holophonic sounds, as he identifies them, are directly registered by the brain without going through the ears. This technique is of great importance in present research with the deaf as well as with general testing being done by audiologists.

Avi Yellin of the department of psychiatry at the University of Minnesota, has developed the skill of letting the heart beat to specific musical rhythms at will. He is able to link parts of the cortex with previously inaccessible parts of the brain. This research is being tested by the National Institute of Health. Although this seems quite distant from any practical use in a music classroom, it may serve to awaken endless possibilities with music therapists as they work with exceptional students.

The Helen Keller model of possibility is available for all of us to awaken to greater knowledge and facility. To peek through a pinhole toward that possibility is now possible. It seems enough, however, to motivate the attention of educators and musicians. This brain bowl, walnut-shaped, reveled and mysterious, is our perception, intuition and agent of communication. It is giving clues to its wholeness. As we come to understand it better, we will be able to break through some of the habits and fears which keep us from participating fully in the great music of creative learning and teaching.

THE MORE CONNECTIONS THAT CAN BE MADE IN THE BRAIN,

THE MORE INTEGRATED THE EXPERIENCE IS WITHIN MEMORY.

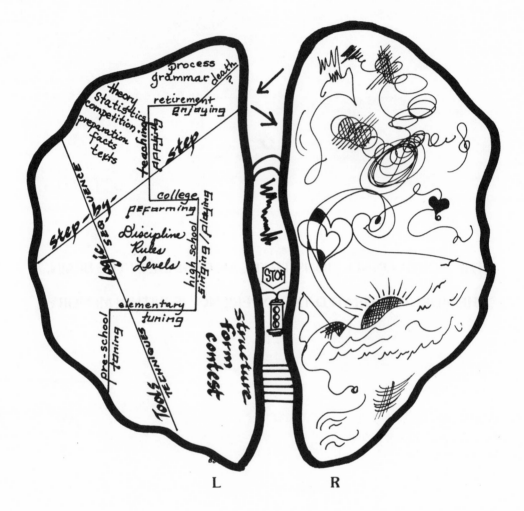

L   R

WHAT'S LEFT FOR US?

Mr. Wright left for work on the right foot, although he was left-handed, drove on the right side of the one-way street, turned left at the wrong place at the right time. His life as a writer was awkward because he could not type and his left-handed slant left skills much to be desired. He wrote on the rites and rituals left to society. He wrote on the rights of human freedom and independence. He wrote on what will be left for future generations' rights.

Mr. Wright left Mrs. Wright even though he was left with the feeling of it not being a completely right decision. Part of him would always be right and he desired to give it right-of-way to his life, no matter what was left.

MORAL: Lobe is a many splintered thing.

Such a painful word play throws our mind into an awkward position, not knowing exactly where it stands. It is similar to an optical illusion or a hall of mirrors where we think we know where we are and where we are going. P.D.Q. Bach uses the run-on musical sentence as a pun in his *Unbegun Symphony*. Just when we think we know the tune, it is suddenly another familiar one. Puns play that role in our language and put us in two or three places of meaning simultaneously. This may not be of great educational importance, but it does lead to an awareness of sight and meaning, not always observable in regular gravitational logic.

As we discuss the informational bits that seem to gravitate to the left hemisphere of the neo-cortex, we should be as logical and straightforward as possible. We no longer need to have a reflective or metaphoric manner to produce associated imagery. We must look closely at the facts. Since the majority of extended research finds the loopholes and exceptions to formally accepted theories, it is impossible to define the left lobe directly. But alas, the key words, the suggested polarity, will be stated with the permission for the reader's left brain to dismiss or accept as he or she chooses.

Our culture is left-brained. The dominance of the logical, grammatical, sequential and timed responsibility for organization to life is shown in the way we teach and the ways in which our students are expected to model.

With the higher forms of educational systems analyzing what has not been taught or experienced, there is an impetus to either reclassify the existing systems or create new ones. John Dewey and Jean Piaget made a powerful impact on our American educational system. In Dewey's 1933 work, *Logic: A Theory of Inquiry,* he analyzed the complete act of sequential and linear thought. It later was referred to as the Scientific Method of Education. Piaget prepared a similar system based on psychological terms in the child's assimilation of logic. Piaget's system divides the child's development into the four following areas:

A. SENSORIMOTOR. This early period exists from birth through age two when most movements take place with little understanding. Only by the feel, sight, smell, sound or taste of an object does the child know it exists. Absolute belief in perceived reality is the child's mental basis and there is no abstract development in thought.

B. PRE-OPERATIONAL. From ages two to five, children begin to use language and start to remember behavior and stimulation from earlier times. Thinking takes place from their own viewpoint, not with the abstraction of anyone else's. They do abstract in the sense of representational actions, motions and imitations.

C. CONCRETE OPERATIONAL. Ages five to twelve bring them to the abstract, logical process. Sensory activity is replaced by speculative and abstract mental duties. They begin to classify and form the rules which have been taught to them. Any deviation from these rules is at fault, not the rule itself.

D. FORMAL OPERATIONS. From age twelve, children are then able to work on two or more abstract thoughts at a time. The youth is now able to become sophisticated enough to observe sequence and consequence to logic, abstract as it may be. One thought relates to another already known and a new one is realized by the mind as a complementary realization.

Piaget's logical theory has been a dominant force in American education. It allowed thousands of other learning theories to absorb its scope and sequence. It was challenged by educators who realized that a child was able to learn faster, earlier and at times out of sequence with his educational scheme. Whether we follow his methodology or not, we are apt to find its potent influence in nearly every school system. His system became more prominent in the 1960's, although it has been researched and written decades earlier. In the same period, educators were writing curriculum for music classes that reflected the learning goals and sequences being prepared by each of the Three-R standards for each grade level. Choral techniques for young choirs dealt with the logical and sequential presentation of each song or anthem. There are scores of "How to Teach Music" books which give all the proper techniques for musical facility without quickening free-form creativity from the child. That is still the prominent method for most church and school choir directors. In other words, musical expression was supposedly taught through teaching skills and singing songs by rote. If there was time at the end of the year, there might be time for creativity. It was not the music teacher or the students who failed; it was simply the ability of our system to expand the center of the creative process within the child. There are exceptions.

But, generally speaking, what is left? A great deal is left and much of it is correct. We now have more music programs, more musicians, more excellent programs throughout the country than probably ever imagined by music educators at the turn of the century. The large choral ensembles and fine competitions all go to refine what this system has brought to us. No doubt we must be organized and logical to have any system work within a social order. Freedom without structure has no place to go.

In speaking of the left-brained, logical sequence in education, Benjamin S. Bloom cannot be ignored. His editorship of the *Taxonomy of Educational Objectives* must be the prime example of the ultra-logic of our left brain schemes. The six following steps in the sequence of the cognitive domain prove this. Thinking, learning and integration take place ideally within these classifications:

1. KNOWLEDGE: of specifics, of ways and means of dealing with specifics, and of the universals and abstractions in the field.

2. COMPREHENSION: its translation, interpretation and extrapolation.

3. APPLICATION: educational implications of objectives in categorical methods.

4. ANALYSIS: of elements, relationships and organization principles.

5. SYNTHESIS: production of a unique communication and a plan or proposed set of operations. Derivation of a set of abstract relations.

6. EVALUATION: judgements in terms of internal evidence and external criteria.

Challenge your pure logic by transposing the above classification to the way a song is taught, the way music is taught from each grade's standpoint, and the way a performance is judged. This should challenge some part of your right brain.

One of the most important values of the left brain/right brain dichotomy is attained through the use and understanding of opposites. Having the permission to use opposites to illustrate contrast and function in the brain somehow soothes part of the left brain crystallization of fixed and rigid belief systems. Opposites provide an alternate metaphor. Eastern philosophy has always included the opposites in balance within the whole. The symbols of the Tao (pronounced Dow) on the Korean flag is one of the most perfect representations of the dual brain:

Two equal raindrops within a circle, the Tao symbol, originated in China. It is divided into halves called *yin* and *yang*. The *yang* is positive, active, hot, potent, stimulating and clear. It is of a lighter color, usually white or red, than the *yin*, which represents the passive, cold, negative, receptive and hazy. Within each of the halves is a small dot of the opposite color representing the fact that all things contain their opposites. As the brain is capable of storing similar bits of information in many places on both sides of the neo-cortex and lower level, the dots in the Tao are a direct implication of Pribram's holographic theory. Although many seeming opposites are actually degrees of measurement of the same quality, it is helpful for the logical part of us to have as many keys for comparative duality as possible. While words such as "high" and "low" are opposite, they have no place in defining the two hemispheric lobes. We will consider the following lists as a logical pattern for the generalizations of opposites and complementaries. These suggestive classifications do not consider their counterparts in the lower areas of the brain, which are essential.

LEFT HEMISPHERE	RIGHT HEMISPHERE
Active	Passive
Light	Darkness
Yang	Yin
Time	Space
Ego	Id
Conscious	Unconscious
Thought	Emotion
Knowledge	Intuition
Robot	Existentialist
Positive	Negative
Verbal	Non-verbal
Reductive	Holistic
Exclusive	Inclusive
Timed	Timeless
Sequential	Diffused
Cognitive	Affective
Words	Sounds
Mathematical thoughts	Artistic impressions
Parts	Whole
Analytical thought	Random feelings
Details	Patterns
Reason	Emotion
Numbers	Geometry

Opposite Natures

Hot	Cold
Dry	Wet
Loud	Soft
Masculine	Feminine
Sun	Moon
Strong	Weak
Continuous	Disconnected
Hard	Soft
Careful	Careless
Specific	General
Happy	Sad
Singular	Plural
Helpful	Useless
Sensitive	Insensitive
Stubborn	Flexible
Mature	Childish
Dependable	Undependable
Beautiful	Ugly
Literal	Metaphoric
Centered	Divergent

It can be seen how different the function is between the understanding of opposites, compared to the hemispheric analogies. These simplistic classifications are not entirely correct although they are convenient. Opposites are always dependent on each other for definition, whereas the state or condition of function is not similarly dependent on another state of varying quality.

It is unwise to think of such information as able to transform education into new modes of function. But it is essential to consider how the lateral polarity will assist in maximizing the creativity of both teachers and students. Although the left hemisphere always seems to be classified as dominant, we must remember that it is easier to test and classify because of its capacity for analytical observation. About ninety percent of society is right-handed, and all but one or two percent, have the language center in the left brain. So, we are left with the unknown variable of possibility in speculating at what the potential of creativity and experience can be in the musical arts. The enjoyment of music and its creative application happen as a result of simultaneous aural perception of sounds, pitches, textures and at times, texts. Our reaction to those perceptions is a simultaneous activity. We are processing it as we experience it. A strong emotional response can form "goose-pimples" during a

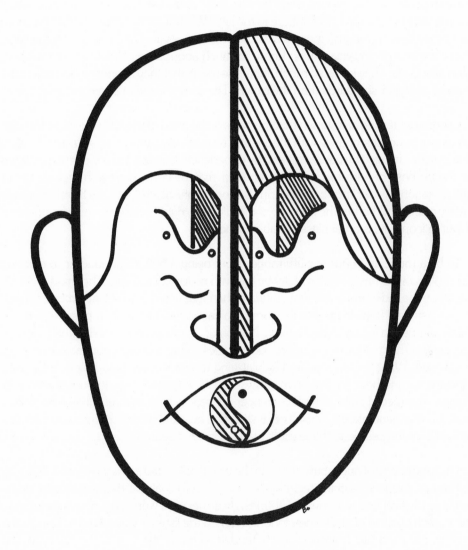

musical experience; yet it is unlikely they will appear for the first time six hours after the listener has heard the music.

When we begin to analyze a piece of music by classifying the instruments, the styles, the compositional techniques and the historical data, we have shifted our musical experience from the right hemisphere to the left. We want to think logically that the more we know about music, the more we will be able to enjoy it. That may not be the case. There are enough musicians who know so much about music that they are unable to listen affectively. They know so much about the music that they cannot enjoy it unless it is of equal of higher standards than their own. The same is true of some music critics.

Laboratory testing has shown that the parts of the brain localized in the lobes through listening experiences, change with the age and musical education of those tested. Musical taste can be changed by education and by experience. One graduate student may listen for the purpose of harmonic analysis, another may be concerned with the manner of interpretation. As our musicality becomes more sophisticated, we can listen on a wide variety of levels. Whether the potency of the affective, right-brained listening is enhanced or put in jeopardy, is an endless variable to judge.

To be a musician in our society ranges from being a brilliant conductor to a young guitar player who has a talent to play by ear with no formal training. The mass of music played on the radio is of a different standard than that heard in recital at a music school. To put taste and knowledge into the same evaluative cauldron is an impossible task. To speak of music in terms of Bach, Willie Nelson or Stockhausen is mixing three diverse languages with simplistic or extensive vocabularies. What is understood may or may not be enjoyed. What is nutritious and exhilarating to one listener may be disruptive and annoying to another. As the brain grows and is educated, the emotional reactions change. The record collection of a teenager appeals to a different emotional need than those of older generations. Therefore, testing and evaluating this is perpetually complex and perhaps impossible in the present stage of brain research.

The asymmetry of audio perception in the brain was tested in the 1960's and 1970's by D. Kimura. Dichotic listening techniques were used to evaluate the hemispheric dominance of musical and non-musical sounds. Two melodies were played simultaneously, one in each channel of stereo headphones. When the listener was asked to identify the melody, the musically trained subjects tended to name the one in the right ear and non-trained listeners the one of the left. Variations of this experiment were done at different age levels and with simple melodies unfamiliar to all the listeners. Asked to sing the dominant melody, both groups tended to sing the melody sung into the left ear. For the most part, the melodies were of similar rhythmic natures so that one did not completely dominate the other. It is curious, although of no significant value in research, to play recordings of elementary partner songs, or pentatonic songs, to children in a classroom situation while they cover one of their ears. Find out for yourself the tune they heard first.

It appears that as musical knowledge grows and listening experience increases, the brain's response to music changes from a holistic experience to a more sequential and linear one. To name and record an experience is still not the same as to enjoy music emotionally. As the brain waves are measured during listening experiences, it is found that the integration of the hemispheric experience and the amount of time for the integration is one of the determining factors of the level of creativity of the person. The consistent integration of both hemispheres in music teaching gives a higher yield in creative experience. This is the basis for the brain games and activities outlined later in this book.

We are left with the belief that, because a student is extensively trained, the creative and musical response has been increased accordingly. We are also looking for the best pedagogical technique for ourselves, assuming that it is therefore the best way to teach all our students. A generalized left-brain music teacher will strive for technical vocabulary and skills as the mans for musical education, but at the cost of creativity. There is no value in being critical of any system. Good teachers integrate intuitively because they experience their subject creatively. That integration is perhaps the most important goal any teacher and musician could have.

Most music teachers and choir directors attempt to fuse their emotional and technical skills into the overall musical experience, but still have a tendency to be wrapped up in competitive performances and production results. The more intuitive nature serves as a backdrop to this activity. To imply that synthesis and change can take place from data and speculation is superficial. Such techniques that grow out of testing the nature of creativity in music through brain research will probably take generations to complete. Yet, the left brain has become attentive to its mate and may now find enough justification to learn from it.

To know the exact location of the learning process in the brain, and how it affects us musically, will probably give us little information on becoming better teachers or musicians. We do know that children learn better in certain conditions and their behavioral patterns prove to be a valid guideline. Whether or not we find claims for new data that prove better learning experience and results, we need not sacrifice what we do have merely to be experimental or susceptible to a new trend that may fade within a few years. The left brain does get caught in debate over what the musical process is. Is it a motor skill, a cognitive process or an emotional echo? We can ask scores of valid, logical questions and quickly convince ourselves to pursue the sometimes vague possibilities of the right hemisphere.

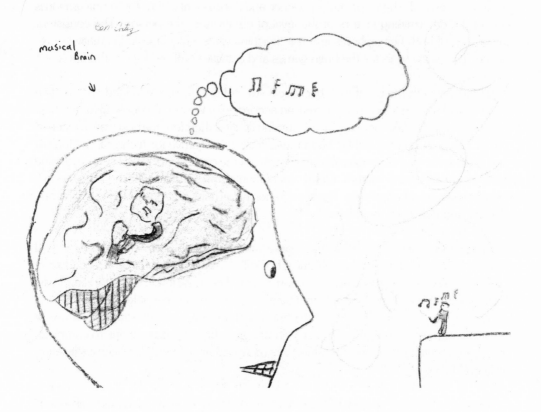

The left brain can serve as its own worst enemy. Until the research therapists have specific and proven data, there is no reason to do anything other than experiment and record. Yet, to experiment without a wide-range awareness of current trends, we do not know what to observe. So much scientific discovery has been made by the seeker who came upon the "new key" by accident. The same could be true with our musical brain research. The "new key" is already working in some public schools in New York without the teacher realizing it. As Pribram speculated about the brain function as a hologram in theory, he later began to find data to prove it. Thus, it is left to us to integrate the sensory techniques of teaching as a possible theory of more creative and whole-brain teaching, take note of the results, and record the data. Within a healthy teaching environment, there is time and opportunity for a teacher to experiment without losing control of the curriculum or students. Take what is known and cycle it to as many creative advantages as possible and not just the logical method. Life is not particularly logical in its daily context, although it may be predictable. The logical researcher will condemn oversimplification. Yet, pedantic overcomplexity is just as dangerous.

To debate over the validity of generalization about musical understanding in hemispheric research is necessary. The criticisms and speculations perhaps represent our own right brain seeking to speak its mind, even in its vocal, non-verbal fashion. To the left brain, the contradiction and inconclusiveness of the opposition on the right brain is almost Aristotelian. The syllogisms do not work in the right brain. In physics, however, the paradoxical nature of the Law of Complementarity suggests that it is through the equal balancing of contradictory natures that wholeness is attained rather than cancelled. Mathematically that would be represented by the following equation:

$+1 - 1 = 0$ logical and Aristotelian

$+1 - 1 =$ the distance between them which inclusively balances at 0. This represents the Law of Complementarity.

It is this manner of inclusive extension that the need for repetition and contrast must go on among researchers and theorists in musical research on the brain. Yes, it is important to know about the ideas of Robert Ornstein's *Psychology of Consciousness* and the researchers included in this bibliography. Perhaps their views and results should all be summarized here, but that is best left to a doctoral student preparing a dissertation, not the kindergarten teacher, choir or band director, or general music teacher.

So what's left for us? It is the suggestion that we approach the tendencies of our right-brained doings, without being inhibited by our left-brained habits and theories, which usually dominate our musical process. To have no plan consciously, is still a plan. To allow the intuitive response and have a vessel to accept it is perhaps the starting point for observation into the other sphere of our creative possibilities.

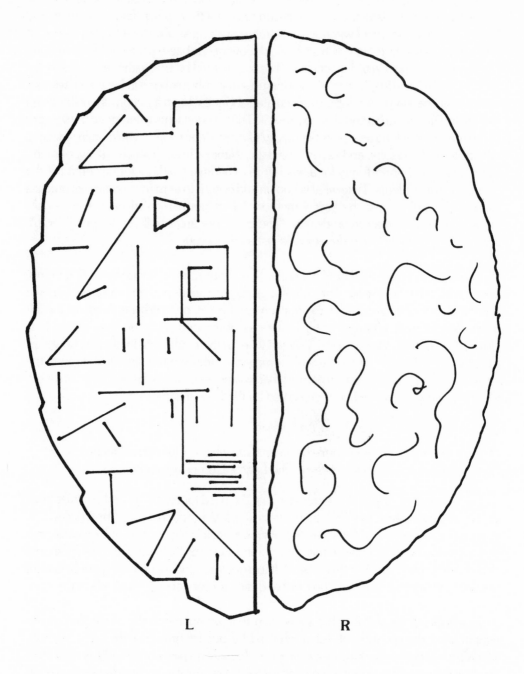

L   R

WHAT'S RIGHT FOR US?

Music is a vital representation of society and culture throughout history. Music grows out of community no matter how primitive or advanced it is. Whether it be communal drum beats encoded as long distance language or chants during rituals of initiation in African tribes, music exists in all human communities. It has expressed spiritual invocations and celebrative dances for weddings. Mothers have lulled their infants with songs, and armies have marched into battle with music. To embrace a right-brained approach to musical development, it is necessary to go back to situations where music education was not formalized or taught as an elective. Folk music was not developed on command by a council or a house of representatives wanting to state or improve a nation's musical status. It evolved out of the natural elements in a community. The religious beliefs, the rites of initiation, the harvests and feast days all brought about the need for musical expression. There is something about music's power to invoke and express that is not found in verbal or written forms.

Both Carl Orff and Zoltan Kodaly were well aware of the psychological search for a universal song in children. Leonard Bernstein spoke of this musical expression as the "basic melody" in his lectures at Harvard University in 1973. An archetypal pattern, which is still obvious in children's songs today, does seem to be at work in melodic developments in the primary phases of many societies.

This universal song has been referred to as the "Ur Song." The Ur language was to have been that language used before the fall of the Tower of Babel. Then language, supposedly diversified and scattered people and confused their ability to communicate verbally. (Genesis 11: 1-9) After people's tongues were confounded, the original language was lost. Ur is a German prefix which means primeval or original.

Bernstein spoke of the "Ur Song" as being a product both of our genetic heritage and the physical laws that determine musical harmony. He said that three notes, *sol, mi* and *la,* were handed to us by nature. Even the respected ethnomusicologist, Bruno Nettl, respects the notion that these intervals are basic to the world's divergent musical development. Through words, games, playing patterns and rhythmic sequences, children all over the world sing this basic song with a variety of rhythms and words. One of the most familiar, using these intervals, incorporates a text haunted with death from the bubonic plagues in England during the 14th century.

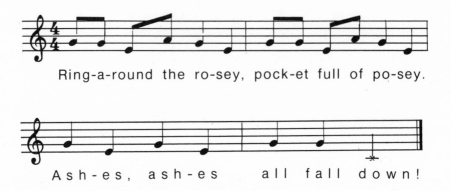

How often we have seen preschoolers in a circle moving clockwise, chanting this familiar ditty and giggling on the last falling note when they plunge to the ground. Amazing it is to see this funny little song as part of their play time, when it reflects one of the most dreaded fears in humanity, death. The text simply states the ring around the rosy (pink sores that appeared with the plague), pocket full of posey (pockets full of flower petals to offset the stench of dying), Ashes, ashes (to dust or burned to dispose of the bodies), We all fall down (We all die).

We find variations of this simple group of intervals, a descending minor third, then an ascending perfect fourth, in hundreds of children's songs. The same pentatonic phrases are used in Japan, China, Europe and North America. Music skills have developed out of symbolic sounds. The earliest sounds that children make are babbling gibberish. This is observed even among the deaf. It is curious to note that most people around small babies tend to chant when speaking to them. "Baby talk" is far more musical than general speech. That the intonation may be more communicative than the words is intuitive. The first musical fragments produced by children occur from the twelfth to fifteenth month. They may not have any tuneful identity, but their undulating patterns over small intervals do show signs of the descending minor third. A quantum leap occurs around the age of one-and-one-half, when children begin to use seconds, thirds and fourths in their singing patterns, although the intervals are not particularly tuned to the musical ear. Most of the melodic "mumbling" before age two and one-half is spontaneous. Then a sense of melodic memory, although fragmentary, begins to occur. They become aware of songs sung in their environment and begin to imitate them rhythmically and melodically. By the end of the third year, the small fragments of "Oink, oink here, oink, oink there" and "Twinkle, twinkle, little star" come together for more musical context so that most of the song can be sung. About age four the learned song assumes dominance over the spontaneous song.

The development of the right-brain musicality in children is basic to the elemental musical approach to Carl Orff. In the 1920's, he and Dorothea Guenther established a school of dance in Munich for the purpose of developing rhythmic education, where music and movements were taught together, supplementing one another. It was hoped that dance students could accompany themselves and learn to make their own music. Initially, there was the need for technically simple instruments that could allow some rhythmic improvisation to take place with simultaneous natural movement. Although there was no knowledge of brain development as we know it today, nor was there much work focused on the young child, Orff did intuitively begin to discover a system for acknowledging the elemental in music.

In 1930, the Ministry of Education in Berlin asked Orff to develop a system of music for the public schools. This never came to pass because of the war, but was revived in 1948. Orff was invited by the Radio Association to do a series of programs for children. Although he no longer taught, he took on the project. "I saw in a flash where rhythmic education ought to be taught. It should be when a child enters school. Actually it should be even earlier, during the preschool years. The unity of music and movement is so naturally present in the child. It is so sadly overlooked that it must be the cornerstone of my present work.[4]

Ironically, Orff's early music in the *Schulwerk,* as the method was called, did not use the singing voice to a great extent. He did not see the possibilities of the Ur Song when he transferred the *Schulwerk* to young children. In its first incarnation, the *Schulwerk,* meaning schoolwork, was designed for college-age students. Orff later came to realize that the child's vocal language, both spoken and sung, held many important keys for his elemental techniques. The natural street songs and games provided important clues for the basic development of rhythm in children. The source of this unity of skills pertaining to the simple, pure and natural musical urges within us, he called *Elemental Music.* "Never music alone, but always connected with movement, dance and speech. It is not to be listened to, but used as a means to communicate." Orff became assured that music born of the natural rhythm of language and the natural rhythm of the body would always communicate.

[4] Carl Orff, *The Schulwerk*

51

After the *Schulwerk* developed, he wrote, "Those who look for a method or ready-made system are rather uncomfortable with the *Schulwerk:* people with the artistic temperament and a flair for improvisation are fascinated by it. They are stimulated by these possibilities inherent in a work which is never quite finished, in flux, and constantly developing."

As the Orff approach developed, it has always maintained the importance of movement, improvisation and rhythmic integration. These are essential to the maintenance of the right brain's natural, and perhaps, elemental vocabulary. To stir the right brain with the logical skills of the left is a potent task.

The zen koan, or riddle, which asks "What is the sound of one hand clapping?" reflects the abstract and irrational mode. The left brain does not feel comfortable with such questions and immediately labels it as absurd. Here is a list of questions which are asked in a typical left-brained manner, but cannot be answered in logical terms. It is metaphoric, full of imagery and aggravating to our linear and logical selves.

? Air

false or true nor false

_____ All music lives in an envelope.
_____ As a thing, music means nothing at all.
_____ Music is the only means of rapid transportation to eternity.
_____ In piano playing, we seldom use our sixth finger because its existence is not physically perceivable.
_____ It's impossible to sing high at sea level unless the ocean is completely calm.
_____ Art is to be hung on the wall, not eaten or sat in.
_____ Everytime it rains in Boston, Beethoven is being played somewhere.
_____ If it's the last subway, walk backwards.
_____ If you cut marble into thin slices, it becomes valuable paper.

Fulfill in the answers

Sound is just vibrations, what about silence? _____
What do you listen to when you are asleep? _____
What do you learn from saying "pull" 673 times? _____
What happens when you use only one ear when you sing? _____
Where do we go from here? _____
What are your questions about these answers? _____

John Cage would use such questions and comments in his books. It is regarded by some as great art and as foolery to others. Our brain centers on a comfortable manner of looking at things. To be able to hear and see in a variety of modes simultaneously is part of the deep creative process. We cannot live only with right brain generalizations in such a world as ours, yet the integration of its non-linear mode seems necessary for our survival.

Looking at things, perceiving them on a number of levels can be summarized by comments written by Leonardo da Vinci in his private notebook:

> I cannot forbear to mention...a new device for study which, although it may seem trivial and almost ludicrous, is nevertheless extremely useful, arousing in the mind various inventions. And this is, when you look at a wall spotted with stains, you may discover a resemblance to various landscapes, beautified with mountains, rivers, rocks or trees. Or again, you may see battles and figures in action, or strange faces and costumes and an endless variety of objects which you could reduce to full, complete and well-drawn forms. And these appear on such walls confusedly, like the sound of bells in whose jangle you may find any name or word you choose to imagine.

Charlie Brown is saying the same thing in one of his conversations with Lucy and Linus while they are lying on their backs looking at the clouds. Lucy asks Linus what he sees with his imagination. He sums up his vision with exotic countries, famous painters and the episode of the stoning of Stephen in the Bible. Lucy then asks Charlie Brown what he saw, and he responds, "Well, I was going to say I saw a ducky and a horsie, but I changed my mind!"

So our mind's eye for the metaphoric and our mind's ear for musical statements change within our own context of the day, hour and situation. We can depend on its changing, we can delight in its timeless response. But what do we do with? It can offend and threaten our logic and our view of the order of things. The age of logic put thinking and being in the same category: "I think, therefore, I am." The left brain mode has defended itself against superstition and non-scientific beliefs.

Artists and poets have taken the visual imagination as an important component in abstract art. Van Gogh and the Impressionists use a right-brained lens on their subjects. Jackson Pollack's vocabulary is exclusively abstract. Painters like Picasso and Klee utilize the power of the abstract to define the real. The left-brain clarity in technical skills in painters like Dali, Magritte and Bosch is contrasted to their symbolic and potent symbolism of the right brain. This technique speaks to more of us at once. It may not bring peace or joy, but it does evoke curiosity and interest. James Joyce grew out of his existing language when he wrote *Finnian's Wake*. With its brilliance, it is still inaccessible to most of the reading public.

In Hugo Ball's poem, *Karawane,* the nonsense, yet logical-sounding words produce a type of secular glossolalia, which makes no sense to read silently. When spoken or sung, metaphoric meaning through rhythm, rhyme and accent of the invented words, a meaning begins to gravitate toward the text.

Some fascinating research has taken place in Japan regarding the localization of functions in the hemispheres. Tadanobu Tsunoda has done an extensive survey on the placement of vowels and language sounds in the brains of westerners, Koreans, Chinese, Japanese, Polynesians and Bengalis. For the most part, vowels are processed on the right side of the brain when they appear alone, and on the left side when they are surrounded by consonants. The Japanese and Polynesians were the exception to this. Their vowels were processed in the left lobe. Mechanical sounds, bells, whistles and machinery were generally processed by all groups in the right hemisphere. Most music in all cultures is processed in the right, yet, the Japanese process their musical language in the left. The Japanese language and the non-verbal sounds used in laughter, stress and music are all in the left, quite an exception to general findings in western brain research. Tsunoda's theory claims the highly vowel centered language, Japanese, without as many diphthongs as English, has caused this to happen. Although his research is not conclusive and has been widely challenged, it is an important and significant inquiry into our quest of understanding mental process.

So, here we are, right in the middle of speculation. The more the right lobe is analyzed, the more the left is in control, consciously. Benjamin Bloom did not stop with his taxonomy of mental domains at the cognitive level; he developed a classification of the affective domain. Because of the acutely analytical nature of his project, even this side of the domain tends to be left-brained. The affective domain is concerned with the attitude, feelings, values and appreciation taking place in the learning process. This begins with: 1. receiving information (looking at it), 2. responding to it (talking or reacting to it), 3. valuing it (trying it out), 4. building it within (emotional organization) and 5. characterizing it (letting it come into personality). Still, organized as this system is, it is worth reflection in musical teaching methods. The left brain is wanting to build the skill and technique while the right brain is wanting to "get on with it" and "go for it" and not spend the time reading or talking about it.

The right brain is a genius in an infant stage. Observation of the variety of data barely tells us what this sleeping giant has in its potential. For what is knows, it needs no proof. It is its own end, no matter how much data is being fed it. It smiles and exudes satisfaction when it is correct, and yet, probably sends out some foggy smoke signals to the left brain, when not being heard. There are suggestions that when the right brain doesn't listen, the body will become ill or imbalanced. Although too assumptive and general is that statement, we do know that ulcers are probably caused by the tensions of emotional

KARAWANE

Hugo Ball, 1917

jolifanto bambla o falli bambla
grossiga m'pfa habla horem

EGIGA GORAMEN

higo bloiko russula huju

hollaka hollala
anlogo bung
blago bung
blago bung
Bosso Fataka

u uu u
schampa wulla wussa olobo

hej tatta gorem
eschige zunbada

wulubu ssubudu uluw ssubudu

Tumba ba-umpf
kusagauma
Ba - umf

impulse contradicting logical information in our minds. When our chemical and electrical brain waves work in harmony in a calm, peaceful environment, we are truly sending out good vibrations.

Biofeedback has given us numerous clues in the learning modes. Music is a potent art form with unlimited power. That Muzak makes it easier for students and industrial workers to perform their duties and that colors and sounds in hospital rooms or classrooms change the mood, perhaps even the mode of learning, should prove that musicians are a part of an important and subtle activity. Over ten years ago a series of tests with plants and music was made in Denver. For a number of weeks, similar types of plants were exposed to Bach, rock and Eastern Indian religious music in a soundproof laboratory. The results were interesting, although not conclusive. The roots and leaves of the plants around the Indian music were larger and healthier than the other groups. The Bach plants were larger than normal plants, while the Rock plants were smaller than normal.

In considering the "right" we find ourselves flung from one topic to another. Knowing that the eyes of the piano students usually gaze upwards to the right when they are looking for a note in their memory (perplexity to the left brain) is curious. This subject of bilateral research is both biological and psychological and it leaves the musician bemused. It seems "too much" to behold. That, in itself, is the dilemma of the right brain study. Its implied gestalt is truly more than the sum of its parts. Even the most prominent researchers, are not surmising that the study of the arts is the only manner of integration for teaching. Yet, the thrust of the brain work has been well stated to educators by Dr. J. E. Bogen of the University of Southern California: "It may be a principle virtue of these more recent findings about the brain, not only to serve as scientific support for a more diversified curriculum, and not only to provide some direction for this diversification, but also to stimulate a new set of questions for those who will pilot the future of education. We have a few new landmarks; hopefully they will help us steer a better course."

In Betty Edward's well-known book, *Drawing on the Right Side of the Brain*, she noted she could either draw or talk, but could not do both at the same time. Both spheres were in competition for dominance. She investigated why some students were natural talents and others had great difficulty in drawing. The talented looked at things differently. She concluded that "an individual's ability to draw was controlled by the ability to shift to a different-from-ordinary way processing visual information from Left mode processing to Right mode processing." After comparing her own process with those of her students, she devised a brilliant process that would allow *anyone* to learn to draw. She described the creative person as "one who can process in new ways the information at hand. Time and time again these individuals have recognized the differences between the two

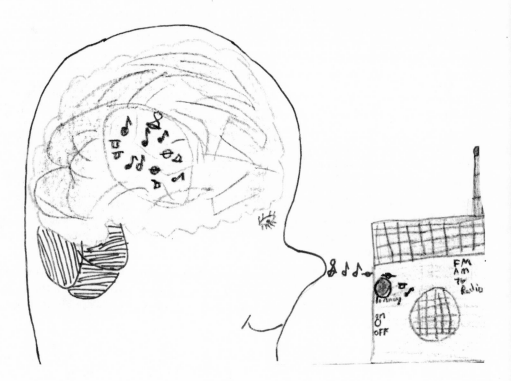

processes which gather information and transform it creatively. Getting to know both sides of the brain is an important step in liberating the creative potential."

Daydreaming and guided imagery in listening are keys to the right of the brain. The familiar stories of how inventors have dreamed their new inventions come from the right mode of thinking. A mental block can be dissolved by doing a non-associated activity like running, doodling, washing the car or improvising music. Music may serve to facilitate the logical studies of our students rather than make them more aesthetically sensitive. History and mathematics may have more to gain from music than our performance techniques. While we are aware that biochemical research has proven that certain foods release important brain chemicals, it is just as possible that music, the sound food, is providing us similar nutrition. Perhaps there is junk music, as there is junk food. Some music is truly not healthy for us, just as the plants responded negatively in laboratory testing. There is also the probability that certain music has no effect on some people and, on the other hand, dynamically brings about peace of mind, even exhilarating religious experiences, with others.

Superlearning techniques are appearing throughout the country. The optimalearning Lozanov method for languages holds a prominent place in the proper and academic scale of relaxed and deep-learning techniques. Children and adults are able to learn languages at an increased rate through the use of imagery, music and an adjustment of the brain waves. It is uncertain that such a catch-all of left brain/right brain techniques is the reason or the new element that allows these systems to work. So what is right for us? Is there a right way to teach or experience music? Is the right part of our brain really a creative friend or a disorganized foe? The left's logic will always caution us not to be unduly infatuated with new trends or simplistic gimmicks for perfecting educational procedures. Yet, with the intuition and the knowledge that we are more than we know ourselves to be, we should more consciously begin to pursue our less verbal lobe in the right frame of mind.

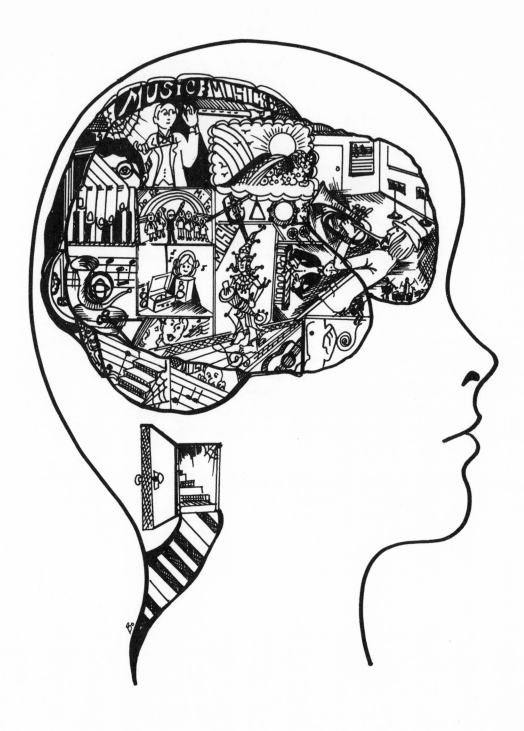

THE MUSICAL CONNECTIONS

Now the most hostile are the most opposite, such as hot and cold, bitter and sweet, moist and dry, and the like. And my ancestor, Asclepius, knowing how to implant friendship and accord in these elements, was the creator of our art (medicine), as our friends the poets here tell us, and I believe them; and not only medicine in every branch, but the arts of gymnastics and husbandry are under his dominion. Anyone who pays the least attention to the subject will also perceive that in *music* there is the same reconciliation of opposites.

Plato, *Symposium*

Saul's servants said to him, "Look, an evil spirit of God is the cause of your terror. Command us, and your servants who wait on you will look for a skilled harpist; when the evil spirit of God troubles you, the harpist will play and you will recover."......And whenever the spirit of God troubled Saul, David took the harp and played; then Saul grew calm, and recovered, and the evil spirit departed from him.

I Samuel, xvi

To modern minds it may make little difference if David was the first music therapist. Whether Orpheus could tame the beasts or David could cure the ill, ancient philosophy and religion did recognize the empowerment of musical arts to bring forth transformation. Did the priests, prophets and shamens before the Renaissance know something about music that is now forgotten?

To recover that which been lost is seemingly irrelevant for the contemporary process in music teaching. To tame a group of seventh graders with the soothing sounds of the harp may work momentarily, but is unlikely to calm their oscillating minds and bodies without a creative ploy.

Music connects us to a subtle emotional response. To search out its meaning in pedagogical systems, therapeutic analysis or simple intuition is an endless quest. The variables of brain research still cannot indicate the source of transformation which deeply affects the listener. The source of creative inspiration in its newness does quicken the response and herein lies the practical connection of music to life.

Music activates the creative imagination within a listener. At times, the event is overpowering and transformative. At other times, there is little response and attention given to listening. To be creative is to develop manners of association which are new. There is an endless flow of curiosity. It lies outside the practical, disciplined and step-by-step manner of expression. Creativity is not dependent on education or qualifications, but on the manner of approach and how things are considered. Creativity takes advantage of the unknown, the unexpected and the peculiar. Being right is not as important as being aware.

The creative impulse comes at its own time. It is difficult to invoke it automatically on Tuesdays at 10:00 a.m. Yet creativity is more than just the new ideas; it is the act of bringing these ideas into form. From the opposites of Plato's thoughts to the different manners of information processing on both sides of the brain, creativity is the bridge between the idea and the form.

Take a moment to answer the following questions which relate to the creative process in yourself. Be a fair judge of yourself and try not to let the practical and correct response overtake the more spontaneous.

Select one answer and insert below.

A. Yes, this is correct most of the time.
B. No, this is not usually my response.
C. I would change my response depending on the situation.
D. I don't know how I would respond.

_____ 1. I am most comfortable when everything is in order.
_____ 2. I work on more than one project at a time.
_____ 3. I like eating at the same time every evening.
_____ 4. I wish the phone would not ring while I'm practicing.
_____ 5. I am slow, but sure.
_____ 6. Ideas come to me out of the blue.
_____ 7. I hear music in my head most of the time.
_____ 8. The potential of an idea is more important than its practicality.
_____ 9. It's of little use to ask questions that have no answer.
_____ 10. I enjoy multiple choice tests.
_____ 11. I'm interested in new techniques of education.
_____ 12. It's boring to listen to the same kind of music each week.
_____ 13. I spend a lot of time getting organized for creative events.
_____ 14. I am more sensitive than most of my associates.
_____ 15. I change my mind often during my creative times.
_____ 16. I often listen to new kinds of music.
_____ 17. In teaching, techniques are more important than inspiration.
_____ 18. I trust my intuition.
_____ 19. I must have time to be alone every week.
_____ 20. Children are more creative than adults.

Creativity can be facilitated in a number of different manners. Through relaxation, the busy modes of thought settle into a more peaceful and receptive state of mind. Through physical activity, the body and mind wake up to new ideas. Through visualization, the mind can virtually walk into new ideas and methods. In the answers you provided for the preceding questions, it was necessary for you to view a situation or segment of your life. The more creative you are, the more possibilities you would see in each of the statements. No one could maintain an absolute routine and be creative. Therefore, such testing is valuable only from the standpoint of self-analysis and awareness. There are no answers to questions of creativity. It is simply the process of surrendering the logical control of the mind and personality to the more spontaneous and engaging awareness of creative thought and action.

Listed below are some rules for creativity as developed through the two modes of operation of the brain. The dual organization makes clear the important aspects of the components of creativity.

Creative Methods cannot insure success	Creative Marvels are exciting and adventurous
organize the experience	flow with ideas
teach the vocabulary	experience, then develop vocabulary
do one thing at a time	allow everything to happen
follow every safe rule	risk what is known
have winning goals	be honest with inner feelings
follow a time sequence	forget time, be absorbed in now
be assertive	listen deeply
co-operate with others	work alone with ideas, then share
be clear	be whatever and start from there
sit still and think	move around until something happens
be serious	be funny
no non-sense	all and every sense
repeat the last creative success	be unusual

Creativity has a dual nature within us. One part tells us how to be creative or gives us permission to be creative. The other part does the creating. If the first part gets in the way of the second, nothing creative seems to happen. If the second part trys to act without the first part, the first will haunt and scold the second. Whether these are actually the two different sides of the neo-cortex or a conglomerate of opposites from the limbic system and the whole cortex, it does not matter. What is important is that the nature of the creative process which has results is balanced. Try, then let go of trying. Compose, then let it compose. Do it, then let it do itself.

It is subtle and difficult for students to let go of structure and process. To let go too quickly can be creative chaos. The tug is endless and has no rational resolution.

Creativity should lure our minds into a manner of living that is consistently interesting. Boredom is a strange malaise of our culture and century. By shortened work weeks and longer lives and retirement, a time for wonderful creativity is provided. But the inner lack of creative education in childhood can cause a physical demise of the mind and body.

Here is a short episode, quite unlikely, most absurd, very creative and perhaps possible:

On February 10, 2025, an ambulance arrived at the General Whole-body Hospital in Prepless, PA. Rushed into the emergency room was Art D. Prived, a 60-year-old male. He had been found completely numb in a polyester shroud on a yellow formica coffee table surrounded by pink plastic flamingos from his front yard. His soul beat was minute, his heart had no feeling and his eyes and ears were shrinking. His left brain was diagnosed with a creeping case of *lassitudo acreativus,* non-creative boredom. His right brain was diagnosed as *amusia in excelsis,* unable to produce or recognize music in the highest. Art was deprived of himself when he was young. He was surrounded by plastic, coupons, twinkies and video machines. He was dying of a lack of beauty, unnatural surroundings and an overdose of instant mashed potatoes.

The hospital was able to revive him in a room full of rainbows, green plants and nurses telling jokes. Every three hours, two preschoolers came from their violin lessons and played for him. His ears grew, his left brain's disease creeped away and his right brain was able to digest solid music. His childhood had been recovered in time to save him from a boring death. He began to carve wood, whistle and paint with his toes. He started to understand jokes and dreamed of new ideas. Art returned home, painted his house and began a folk dance society.

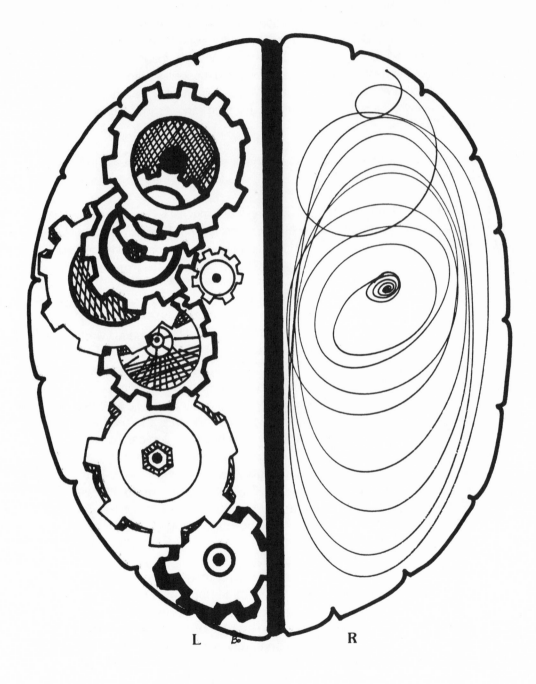

L   R

The same thing happens today with many practical results. Music helps thousands of retired people through folk dancing, handbell organizations, crafts and meaningful exercises that keep the brain and body active. Music transcends entertainment and a passive occupation when the elements of thought, action and cooperation are taking place. Creativity is reawakened by stimulating the minds with as many multi-sensory experiences as possible. Whether creativity is geriatric or pre-primer in nature, it heals! Healing is the process of becoming whole, more than what was. The musical connections to the psyche of the body are deep and should be attended throughout life.

Habits often educate the physical body with imbalance and stress. To constantly awaken old habits within a new framework activates creative thinking. As children begin to form their habits of action and thought, the introduction of creative alternatives is easier then, than at any other time of life. Good habits can be expanded and poor habits can be altered. For example, the use of kinesthetic awareness and skills readily improves memory and actions.

Kinesthesia is the awareness of what the body is doing. Acute attention is given to the movement of muscles and the breath. The sensory perception of one finger while playing a familiar piece on the piano will begin this awareness. By turning off one part of the automatic function and replacing it with concentrated awareness imposes a new memory. (See the exercise "Mental Keyboards" in the last chapter.)

Moshe Feldenkrais has done extensive research in this area. His exercises and techniques for re-educating the body and brain are of tremendous importance to educators. When the motor neurons are activated in a variation of a habit and the tendency is relearned, awareness is improved and greater fluidity of movement occurs. Unlock your car with your non-dominant hand. Dial the telephone with the non-dominant hand.

Feldenkrais speaks of this observation in his book, *Awareness Through Movement:*
> The execution of an action by no means proves what we know, even superficially, what we are doing or how we do it. If we attempt to carry out an action with awareness — that is, to follow it in detail — we sooner discover that even the simplest and most common of actions, such as getting up from a chair, is a mystery, and that we have no idea at all of how it is done. Do we contract the muscles of the stomach or the back, do we tense the legs first, or tilt the body forward first, what do the eyes do, or the head? It is easy to demonstrate that a man does not know what he is doing, right down to being unable to rise from a chair. He therefore has no choice but to return to his accustomed method, which is to give himself the order to get up and to leave it to the specialized organizations within himself to carry out the actions as it pleases them, which means as he usually does.

Kinesthetic awareness begins to activate the image of the action which can be remembered both in the mind and the body. The body seeks to balance itself. When there is a dysfunction in the cortex, be it pain or stress, the body can effectively balance itself through motor activities which stimulate the lower areas of the brain. A baby cries, he/she is rocked, the limbic system is lulled. By clapping, turning and spinning a remediation occurs. By being aware of the kinesthetic movement, the action can be visualized and balance can occur. Language and verbal skills readily improve when these creative and practical techniques are employed.

The present is an era for pioneering musical potential. What has been regarded as avant-garde and irrational may provide the blending agents for in-depth balanced learning. No doubt, the musician may feel like it is a great threat to approach performance and teaching with these new tools. But it is not so challenging to the old habits if creativity has been a partner in past musical experiences.

The next time a surge of hemi-demi boredom or lethargic creativity comes along, try a couple of the following to see if some musical connections can be made.

- jog backwards for five minutes

- clean out the garage while whistling themes of Beethoven

- jump rope and make a decree of wishes

- close the eyes and surround your body with a radiant purple light

- doodle for ten minutes with your non-dominant hand

- breathe deeply and think of your favorite foods

- turn on the radio and dance like a six-year-old

- daydream in different parts of your brain

- explain why you are bored to a bowl of yellow jello

photo by Richard S. Orton

PUTTING OUR HEADS TOGETHER: WHOLE MUSICIANS

Grown-ups love figures. When you tell them that you have made a new friend, they never ask you any questions about essential matters. They never say to you, "What does his voice sound like? What game does he love best? Does he collect butterflies?"

Instead, they demand: "How old is he? How many brothers has he? How much does he weigh? How much money does his father make?" Only from figures do they think they have learned anything about him.

from *The Little Prince*
St. Exupéry

Is it only from statistics that we can value our systems of music in education? The Little Prince, with his perfect intuition and unknown skills in either bilateral thinking or holographic brain concepts, puts our plight back in perspective. "Only from figures do they think they have learned anything about him." Could we bend that phrase into the personal and subjective, "Only from our figures do we think we have learned anything from ourselves?"

In 1968, a potent and popular book on education was published. *Education and Ecstasy*, by George B. Leonard, quickened educators to look at the process, means and manners of what was happening in our schools. He spoke of the brain, of the artist, of the child. His ideas were potent and exact with relevance to the plight and frustration of the teacher. Finally, he challenged us with three basic ideas: 1. That human potential is infinitely greater than we have been led to believe. 2. That learning is sheer delight. 3. Learning is life's ultimate purpose.

These have enormous implications and create enormous questions in regard to our values and processes. As a statement of future possibility, he ends his book with the following paragraph:

> Every child, every person can delight from learning. A new education is
> already here, thrusting up in spite of every barrier we have been able to build.
> Why not help it happen?

That statement is as purposeful now as it was when written and will continue to be so for future generations. Since the time it was written, great steps have been taken toward making it happen. The signs and interests are apparent and our new keys to the brain are preparing us for more and more security in letting the learning process be creative, enlightening and fun. Yet, many teachers have found that the enthusiastic surge of creative joy in the classroom and choir room has left. Enthusiasm has been replaced by standard repetition and contrast. How many music teachers have voluntarily taken on third grade classroom teaching or another job? How many people working with computers are of the musical alumni? How many teachers realize that their jobs are in jeopardy because of finances and are forced to either dilute their programs, to take on the teaching of another subject or to move into an administrative position? Something has run amuck in our musical philosophy and purpose. If music has potential, have we been able to integrate it into the lives of our students to such a point that its daily and weekly survival in schools is not under the threat of dismissal? Surely the pain of these facts and possibilities should not keep us from getting on with the potential we have. 'Tis easy to speculate and yet most difficult to find viable means to carry out these possibilities. George Leonard did not leave his questions at rest in *Education and Ecstasy*. He continued his quest for educational and social means of growth through remarkable research which is recorded in his later books: *The Man & Woman Thing and Other Provocations, The Transformation: A Guide to the Inevitable Changes in Humankind,* and the *Ultimate Athlete.* In 1978, he published *The Silent Pulse,* a book which searches for the perfected inner rhythms and music of every person. The quest led him to music, not simply music of elementary education, but to the fundamental pulses in our inner harmonies. He discusses the brain, the senses and the increased ability of each of us to enter the education of each moment. True, here we are treading on the abyss of right-brained fogginess, but we are closer to its creative power than ever before as a profession. We have more to gain than to lose in striving for the wholeness of our potential.

Lorin Hollander has not been shy to speak of his ecstacy in music education and working with piano students in their adventures with it. At a recent festival in the midwest, he delivered an extemporaneous speech which did not avoid the potent spiritual nature of what music is. "When I was a little baby, I would go to the piano and all morning I would choose which note I would become. I would go to the keyboard, reach usually for E-flat. I pushed the E-flat and I would become E-flat. I would resonate E-flat. Every feeling, every fiber in my body would become E-flat. There was nothing else but E-flat. And the world would appear differently to me. Then I would decide where I would go from E-flat. Some days I would try the G-natural, and I would spend the whole day laughing, giggling and rolling on the floor. One day I played G-natural and then decided to take the terribly daring step of going from G-natural to G-flat. Now, you try this step, play an E-flat chord, major, and listen as you've never listened before. Become E-flat major, feel it tickle the body internally, then play G-flat and every desperate, terror-stricken, anger-ridden moment in your life will become that experience. There is a key there to the human emotions far more exact than any human understanding of the psychological sciences have brought forth. We are dealing here with what is still unknown or not recently rediscovered." It is this ultimate absorption known to children and masters of music that give us the power to know what music is about. Hollander continues: "Mozart was a Mason. He dealt with his mysteries in a society. Beethoven we can't say was a deeply religious person, but he was a believer. Bach wrote every note out of a love for God. Schubert was one of the gentlest souls who ever walked the earth; Haydn also. People gather around this energy. People hover around artists who have tapped this energy. All of us as children had it. Many of us have regained it."

This power is truly the basis of our possibilities in whole brain work as musicians. THE GOAL IS TO USE OPTIMAL CREATIVE EXPERIENCES TO ENHANCE THAT WHICH CHILDREN HAVE NATURALLY, NOT TO ENTERTAIN THEM AND ARTICULATE SIMPLY A LOGICAL FORM OF MUSICAL VOCABULARY. To assist adults in remembering their childlike senses is to allow them to regain music as a form of empowerment and health.

Holistic trends seem to imply to many people the leftover psychology from the late 1960's when the flower people were calling for peace in front of society. Holistic implies to others a way of eating and keeping the body in natural and balanced health. Musicians do not classify themselves into these categories of health and psychology. The divisions rest on the type of music that is preferred and performed. The sense of holistic relevance can be classified in religious, social, psychological and neurobiological terms, but not in musical terms until the awareness of music's elemental connection to all of life's rhythm is observed from a deep well of our elemental memory. That experience can be compared to the holy, the spirit-filled, the complete gestalt or zenith of awareness and function. To approach a whole musical experience is perhaps too extreme for those who teach twelve classes of general music a day or just have one children's choir rehearsal a week. It may be too extreme for that half-hour a week we have to ourselves for deep and relaxed listening. As one seeks to be a whole musician, quickened with the joy and depth of making and listening to music, one finds meaning whether there are words to define that experience or not. Our wholeness already exists and cannot die, but it can be forgotten. A routine can fog our consciousness so that nothing feels new. Step-by-step, that consciousness of the thrill of music loses its potency with emotional and physical strain. The holistic key is one of constant awareness, not just knowledge, of the exciting and wonderful creative dance that exists in all life. No one can maintain it for us.

Our brains are mysterious, full of ancient memories and forms and new possibilities for ages to come. No moment can be boring if we are aware of the life-dance that is singing around us. The sense of *AHA!*, the fullness of creation as an act of pure musicianship is the only introduction there is to the musical brain. We felt it as children, we studied it as youth and now we pass it on to others. We have been introduced to our musical brain, but we have not always named it, or we have named it so many names that we forget its basic definition. It is right within us, ready to surge and integrate with all the other forces of the senses. Let's put our heads together, now, while the arts are still a part of our educational society.

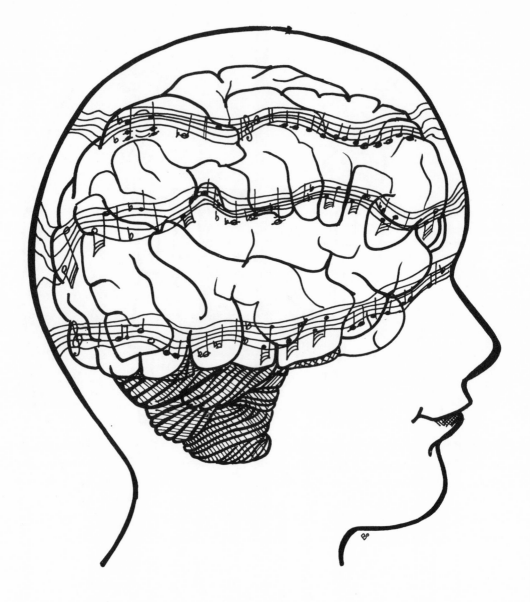

HUM-DRUM EXERCISES

The last thing a musician wants to do is philosophize. A musician is one who makes music. That is pure and simple. It is for the musicologists, the music therapists and the aesthetic philosophers to spend their time in speculation about the nature of music. All the discussion and theories of process are not going to produce one note of music. Bach speaks far louder in his music than all the philosophical discussions of music have in the past. Our musicianship and the ability to communicate it through performance or a learning or listening experience is the bottom line for the evaluation of the art. This book does not intend to reach far from the area of speculation. It presents a collage of thoughts, facts and theories for the purpose of expanding our musical quest. WORDS FAIL TO BE MUSIC.

Approximately one hundred and fifty exercises have been tested with children and adults with the hemispheric response in mind. Of those, some of the most dramatic for sensory integration have been recorded in the exercises that follow. Some may be quite new in concept with their kinesthetic and image-making techniques. Some may be slight variations of familiar exercises. Others may be small gimmicks for one time use and amusement.

These exercises are a concise review for those who have experienced them in workshops and classes. The exercises which deal with visualization, kinesthetic movement and memory techniques need to be experienced by the teacher BEFORE the teacher attempts to use the exercise with a group. Some of the exercises are quite simple and can be easily translated from the printed page to the musical experience. Most of the exercises can be adapted for use at any age.

HUM - DRUM? Boring? No, just the opposite! The goal is to provide multisensory learning experiences to utilize as much of the motor and sensory parts of the cortex as possible. The implications show that skills in reading and mathematics improve through the use of integrated arts. To hum and drum at the same time while tap dancing, chewing salt water taffy and listening to a French lesson on a set of headphones may just facilitate the decrystalization of some of our tightened logic in fine art education and create a more valuable learning environment. The present stage may seem like it is full of faddish techniques, yet we know that they do lead to undeniable improvement in the overall education of a child. When an artist as an educator can reach the child in today's world, the patronage of our profession will not be in jeopardy. Children's games and Bach need not be strangers, but partners in the great dance of learning.

Tell me

Show me

Involve me

TELL ME, I'LL FORGET

SHOW ME, I MAY REMEMBER

INVOLVE ME, I'LL UNDERSTAND

An Old Chinese Proverb

BEING THE MUSICAL BRAIN

GROUP EXERCISE

for 20 or more persons

IMPORTANT NOTE: The leader of this exercise should have the majority of the information and sequence memorized. Eye contact with the members of the brain circle is essential. The impact of learning is not as effective when read. The leader should move within the circle freely. Note that these generalizations of the left and right hemispheres are NOT solid boundaries and are oversimplified for the purpose of introducing the materials.

BEING THE MUSICAL BRAIN

Have all the participants stand in a circle. Explain to them that you are introducing them to the neo-cortex or upper layers of their brain.

The two hemispheres have generally different ways of processing and acknowledging information. As the circle is split into two lobes, the leader introduces the two contrasting natures to each other:

"Hello, Left Brain! You are clear and logical. Full of order and clarity, you are the one that can clearly speak what's on your mind. You are to the point, direct and exact. You want to do things in the correct order at the very right time. You respond immediately without wasting a word. Every time I acknowledge you, please respond in a prompt, left brain way by saying 'Hel-lo.' As you speak this in a firm military voice, stand at attention and make a brief marching motion. So, 'Hello, Left Brain!!!' (response) 'HEL-LO'. "

Now turn to the other side of the circle and speak in a more gentle and mellow voice:

"Well, hi, Right Brain. How are you feeling?

"You are full of ideas, sounds and expressions that cannot put themselves into words. You know it is now and are not so interested in the past or the future. It seems a lot more

relaxed over here and not so full of structure and organization. You like to respond but don't have the words. Every time I acknowledge you, respond with a brief butterfly dance and wiggle your tongue and let many different pitches be made going up and down the scale. Let's try it. 'Hello, Right Brain!' (response) 'A, la, bi, bah, mi, ba, lee, lee.'"

(turning to the left lobe and speaking in a direct and stern manner)

"Now WHAT are you laughing at? We are here on business to learn directly about the brain. We are not here to be entertained. So...'HELLO, Left Brain!' (response) 'HEL-LO' That's better."

"We are here to make a point and find better definitions to help us understand our brains better. This will assist in our technical abilities as musicians, especially to read and remember important data. This left brain understands how important it is to articulate musical expression. You know how to read, you know the letters. You know how to spell and put the proper tense into the verbs. You seem to be in control of most of the I.Q. since you know how to be logical on the examinations. You know C-O-W, cow. You know that is the animal that gives us milk. You know how to describe its physical features and that many of them live in Wisconsin."

(to the right brain, as the leader is on hands and knees)

"MOOOOOOOOOOOOOOOO."

*"Over here we can't name it, but we know what it sounds like, what it looks like and what its nature is. Oh, yes, right brain, you somehow understand the cow, even though you cannot spell it, look it up in an encyclopedia or give much data about it. You **are** MOOOOOOOOOOOOOOOOO. 'Hello, Right Brain!'"*

(suddenly)

"Hello, Left Brain."

(suddenly)

"Hello, Right Brain. Excuse me, but the left brain needs attention and to have its interest perked up. It gets bored very quickly at times and then becomes critical. I don't want to have it gripe at me. I know you understand. The left brain probably gripes at you sometime because you just aren't organized in the same way it is. You are so different. You may not seem to be on time when the left brain wants you to be creative. I know...sometimes you want to be left alone for a while and just let your artistic ideas

"Hello, Left Brain!"

flow. It does feel good to be over here with some of your visions,sights, inspiration and sounds. You just wish you could express them more often without all that critical response from the left. You really have those wonderful moods of compassion, joy, love and mercy."

(turning to the left)

"Hello Left Brain" (response) 'HEL-LO'

"O.K., Let's get back to business. You know that all of that over on the right is important, but you also know how essential it is to be responsive and clear in this world. Yes, compassion is important at its proper moment in the right context, but it won't get you through school, will it? You wish more of the professors had it, but you don't really have enough time to develop the appropriate theory of compassionate actions."

(turning to the right)

"Ah...it's so simple over here. We may not have any place to go, but it's just more fun to be here. Improvisation is a more honest expression...'Hello Right Brain'...it just brings expression into the now. Sometimes our expressions don't make too much sense to the

other side, but it is really quite honest. If only we could express this part of our minds more often."

(still to the right)

"It's here that music seems to localize and be integrated in the brain. It's listening enjoyment and participation that is natural to everyone. When the right brain is young, it listens to all sorts of music and enjoys most of it."

(to the left)

"We can truly understand the important and essential nature of the left brain and its use for our aesthetic growth, yet without the proper vocabulary and technical tools of that expression, we could never be artists. We must teach our students to be keen on reading and performing music in the most perfect form possible."

(to the right)

"Oh, but music is to feel the flow of life and the beauty of all creation without sound. We get all involved in the non-musical things over on the left...it's so much more expressive here."

(to the left)

"But without the proper scope and sequence, music and all the arts just become emotional mush and we all KNOW how senseless that is."

(to the right)

"...whistle and sing. Oh, we don't bother with all that, it's too far away from...the beauty of singing. (begin to sing a song without any text)

(Leader now comes back to the center and talks to both brains.)

"The Left and Right brains really don't operate in such a generalized fashion, but they do have these tendencies which serve our purpose here. We all have similar tugs within ourselves between our intuition and knowledge. Some of us are far more dominant in our logical process and some of us are more at home with our improvisational and immediate responses. We all know that it is the combination of both these tendencies that brings us into a ripe and meaningful teaching experience. We know that the localization in the hemispheres of the music process begins on the right side and for most people stays there throughout their lives. The exception to that is with musicians. As the educated musician develops more technical skills in reading music, notating music, its styles and possibilities in performance, the dominance changes to the left hemisphere. The purpose of our simple brain-mapping here is to show the need for a balanced attention to these polarities in our music process."

You can simplify this experience for your younger children and add many more musical experiences."

(suddenly to the right)

"Hello, Right Brain..."

"Don't worry, which I know you don't. We are not going back into our logical side entirely. I want to tell you a little about your motor skills. The right side of the brain, for the most part, rules the left side of the body. With the exception of your eyes, ears, nose and tongue, most of the opposite side of your body is ruled by you. So Right Brain, you are the left side of your body. Now take a moment to let just that part of your body, flutter like a butterfly, yet without any rigid or abrupt movements. It can be fluid and flowing or it can be carbonated and bubbly. Make sounds as you move the left side of your body."

(to the left)

"Yes, it is quite logical that you, Left Brain, do rule the right side of the body. Begin to move the right side of yourselves with angular and direct motions. March with your right foot, make angular motions with your right arm and wink at me in a constant rhythm with your right eye while you sing a march."

(to both sides)

"Let's put our heads and motor skills together. Everyone march with the right side of your body and flow and glide with the left side of your body. It's all right, you left-brained people who are also left-handed, this exercise won't hurt you at all. Half the body is rigid and the other half is flowing. Walk around the room within the area of our brain-map while doing both of these types of motions. When you are in the right brain section, make right brain sounds, and when you are in the left brain area, speak rhythmically."

"Begin"

(Let this continue about two minutes, then ask the brains to reverse sides of the body. Continue that for one minute.)

"Hello, Right Brain!"

(to everyone)

"Go back to your first position in your left or right lobe. Now find a partner from the other side and have a conversation with the other side of the brain. The people in the left lobe use words those in the right lobe, use sounds and motions. Really try to communicate with each other. It's a two-way charade. After two minutes, you will change roles. Now find the other half of your brain and begin."

(After two minutes with each person as one side of the brain, have everyone lie comfortably on their backs or sit comfortably in their chairs.)

"Now we will put our bodies and brains in a comfortable and relaxed position, breathing deeply and naturally. Think about these experiences you have had during this exercise. Can you think about it in a different manner than you are used to thinking? Concentrate on the right side of your brain. Imagine it filling with enlightenment and intelligence in a very pure form. We could call it the perfect intuition. As you inhale, fill this right side of your brain with this perfect intuition. Some soft music will be played. There is no need to pay any attention to it with your musical intelligence. Just let it fall into the background of this experience."

"Begin to breathe gently and deeply and relax."

(Begin soft music. Barber's "Adagio For Strings" is suitable.)

"As your right brain is filled with enlightenment and relaxation, I will serve as your left brain and make some simple suggestions about what we have experienced in the last hour. Remember you are thinking with your right side, so there are no words to talk about the experience. There is no time to value or compare the experience. There are only symbols, sounds, pictures, essences of ideas and gentle moods to reflect. Stay in your right mind. When logical questions and observations come into view, don't try to push them out, just let them float by without paying a great deal of attention to them."

(allow at least 30 seconds of silence to pass before continuing)

"Remember looking across the room to a friend who was on the other side of the brain. Recall their actions and responses."

(30 seconds)

"Recall a moment when you felt you had learned something important in your music teaching through one of these techniques."

(30 seconds)

"Recall a time when you felt uncomfortable during some part of the exercise. Let your right brain explain why you felt that way.
(after thirty or forty seconds)
Now let the right brain tell you it's all right to feel that way."

(20 seconds)

"Recall a time when your brains were having a tug-of-war over how to teach a song."

(20 seconds)

"Ask your right brain how it would teach if the left brain were not in control."

(20 seconds)

"Ask your right brain if it would try to communicate more to the left."

(20 seconds)

"Now as you continue to relax and breath deeply, awaken the left brain. Let it's personality come through and let it acknowledge the right brain as its perfect complement. Let the right brain acknowledge the same of the left brain."

(30 seconds)

"Let them find ways that they are balanced with each other"

(30 seconds)

"Our goal is to think and experience with the whole brain as one harmonic and coordinated being. Our generalizations of the hemispheres is just an exercise for balancing our dominant natures with their complementary opposites. Take a moment and think of which opposites would help you fulfill your potential in music teaching."

(1 minute)

"By the integration of our sensory experiences, we can unite our complements. When you are angry, take fifteen minutes and dance it out with the non-dominant part of your body. When you need an idea for teaching or dealing with a special person, take some time and dance it with the acknowledgement of your non-logical brain. This is the beginning to becoming *more* whole. We never reach our potential, but such techniques are essential for ourselves as teachers and our students as they seek to find healthy and complete expressions in their lives."

"As you remain relaxed, slowly begin to stretch."

(30 seconds)

"Open your eyes and be aware of this room. Slowly begin to move and breath deeply."

(1 minute)

"It is a good time to improvise, sing or practice a skill that needs improvement. You may draw your impressions of your own brain or write about some new ideas that came into your mind."

(play soft Baroque music during this activity time)

A BRAIN DANCE

Group Exercise
For all ages

This exercise is for the stimulation of the non-dominant part of the body. The left-handed participants should do the exercise with the right part of their body and the right-handed participants should use the left part of their body. It is essential for the room area to be open so that movement can easily take place.

Exercise, Activity
The Non-Dominant Dance

Music:			
	"Champagne Polka"	Johann Strauss	Columbia M30677
	"The Moldau"	Smetana	
	"España"	Chabrier	Columbia M30383

Begin with the left hand (non-dominant hand) with every possible motion as it moves with the music. Suggest that each finger be an independent dancer with much concentration given to the third and fourth fingers. Gradually extend the movement to the wrist, arm and elbow. Remind the participants that the dominant side of their body is to remain motionless.

The dancing hand and arms can conduct and dance with every creative variation possible. The more parts of the non-dominant part of the body that are being added do not detract from the activity in the hand. Add the toes, foot and ankle on that side of the body and suggest that all parts of the left side of the body begin to dance.

Suggest that the tongue begin to dance on the left side of the mouth and constantly remind the dancers of their hips, fingers, toes, cheeks and elbows.

Approximately three-fourths of the way through the selection add the opposite side of the body in a full body movement throughout the room.

After this stimulating exercise, ask the participants how they feel. Notice the differences between the feelings in the left and right hands. If drawing material is available, request that they draw their feelings with the non-dominant hand and then with their dominant hand.

This exercise is of use to keyboard teachers for developing the weaker hand of students.

3—6—9

Game & Activity
for partners and groups
Age 8 - adult

This game can be played very easily with just the first steps being learned, or in a long-range sequence of advanced steps. Its purpose is to activate the rhythmic, verbal and tactile skills simultaneously. Through the use of many polyrhythmic elements, the brain is stimulated. Speaking in a duple meter, clapping in a triple meter, the use of playful language and the use of an additional beat per sequence allows a variety of skills to be experienced simultaneously. It is truly easier to do than to think about doing it!

This clapping and speaking game is a variant on a familiar children's game chant. Its multi-levels of rhythmic and physical sensory skills are an essential tool for awakening different parts of the neo-cortex and the sensory and motor homunculi.

Have the participants stand in a circle. Begin to speak the phrases below in rhythm while walking clockwise around the circle and looking at the participants. After each phrase, all the participants should echo the phrase:

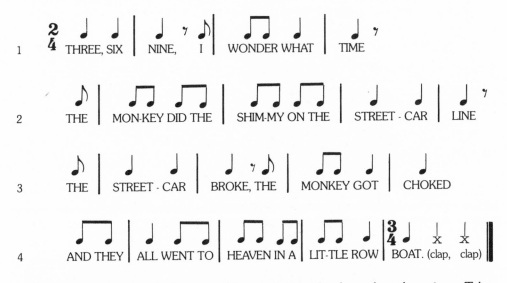

Repeat this echo of each phrase until the whole chant has been done three times. Take special note of the last measure. It has three beats and ends on two claps. It is essential that there is not an extra beat added between the last clap and the first beat on the the word, "Three." This throws the natural accent in the duple meter out of line. This is crucial to the effectiveness of the exercise.

The leader should then change the walking direction. Without losing a beat, the leader should begin to speak lines one through two while walking in a counterclockwise direction. The participants then echo the first two lines before the leader continues with the last two lines. Although the normal tendency of some of the participants is to add a beat after the clap, the leader will continue to keep the correct rhythm pattern. It is helpful for the leader to raise two fingers in the air at the beginning of the final line, so as to remind the participants that they will clap twice.

After this complete chant is learned, ask each person to quickly find a partner. Whoever is left over becomes the leader's partner. Begin to teach the following clapping sequences.

CLAPPING SEQUENCE #1
A. Palms down on the front of the thighs   beat 1

B. A normal, palm-to-palm clap   beat 2

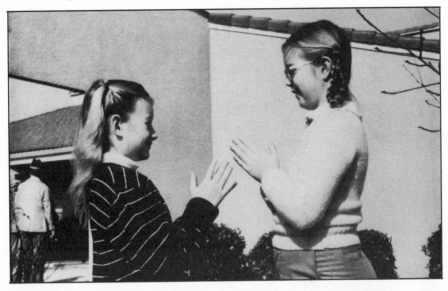

C. With partner, clap across your left palm to his right palm   beat 3

This mirror-like clapping is quite easy and is learned by everyone after a couple of tries. While this is going on, begin the chant, 3 - 6 - 9. The two claps at the end of the chant are always done, no matter where the particpants are in their groups of three. (They should all be at the same place, but there are some very interesting variations.) After the two claps in the chant, without adding an extra beat, repeat the chant with clapping sequence #1. Here we have a verbal duple and a clapping triple. Do not tell the participants what they are doing at this point. After three full repetitions of sequence #1, go to sequence #2.

CLAPPING SEQUENCE #2
A. Palms down on thighs, as before
B. A normal clap, as before
C. Everyone puts his/her left palm up, horizontally.

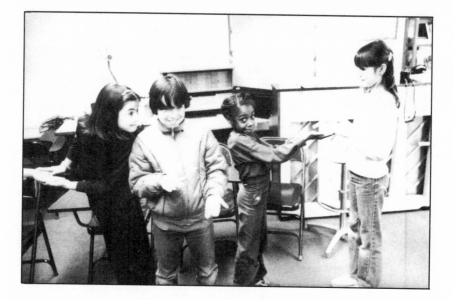

The right palm is down. Move your hands so that they are now able to clap with your partner's in that position.

Now begin to do these three steps as "3 - 6 - 9" is being chanted. Do this sequence three or four times. Be sure that the participants are still standing in a circle with their partners.

CLAPPING SEQUENCE #3
A. Same as previous step A
B. Same as previous step B
C. This time we will begin to alternate the palm that is up. In other words, the first time, you will all have your right palm up, then you will go back to the left, then right, and so forth.

There is usually a lot of laughter and happy frustration with this sequence. Sequence #1 is completely mirrored and balanced. What the eye sees is what the eye does. The motor homunculus does not have to rectify any of the physical motions observed by the sensory homunculus. In sequence #2, the brain has to learn the variation. It is easier to simply show the group step three of sequence #2 and have them repeat it 6 times. It is memorized in the body rather than in the logical mind. Finally in sequence #3, the mind has to think. It must remember to change every third beat. Alas, challenge!

Some participants may not be able to do it and frustration sets in after a couple of attempts. The leader should make a suggestion that the participants should look at their partner's ear or nose rather than the hands. This puts the hands in the peripheral vision rather than in the center of focused vision. The brain processes the information more quickly in this way.

This is usually the stopping point for this exercise for one class. It is interesting to note that children will continue to do this exercise outside of the class until it is perfected. When there is a mistake, laughter heals it. The challenge is fun. There are fifty more sequences in this. A few more are explained below.

As Jean Houston would say, this is a "polyphrenic" exercise. We are using our senses of touching, hearing and seeing. We are clapping in a triple meter, speaking a duple meter, using a text that is silly and illogical. The extra clap keeps the rhythm from being regular. We are using more areas of the brain than in many normal activities.

CLAPPING SEQUENCE #4
A. As before
B. As before
C. As before, with the alternation of palms up as in sequence #3, part C.
D. The clapping sequence now becomes a 4/4 pattern rather than a 3/4 pattern. After the palm that is down has horizontally clapped the partner's palm, it moves upwards and claps the palm that was the partner's downward palm.

This alternates as happens in step C. What seems more difficult is actually quite easy because of the change in rhythm. There is still that added clap at the end.

CLAPPING SEQUENCE #5
A. Go back to sequence #1 and repeat it with the partner.
B. In the two claps that follow the chant, have everyone in the circle turn around 180 degrees, so that they have a new partner. (Note that partners cannot have their backs to the walls of the room or to the center of the circle. They must be facing their partners and still keeping only one circle.) Continue with sequence #1 with your new partner.
C. On the two claps at the end of that, turn so that everyone is facing toward the center of the circle. Continue by doing sequence #1. The third step is then done with the people on both sides.
D. On the two claps at the end of step B, turn with your back toward the center of the circle and repeat it.

CLAPPING SEQUENCE #6
A. Repeat sequence #2 with partner.
B. Repeat the same steps in sequence #5 with the left palm up. With your partner, with your neighbor, facing center and then with back to the center.

CLAPPING SEQUENCE #7
A. Repeat sequence #3 with partner.
B. Repeat the same steps in sequence #5 with alternating palms. With your partner, with your neighbor, facing center and then with your back to the center.

CLAPPING SEQUENCE #8
A. Repeat sequence #4 with partner.
B. Repeat the same steps in sequence #5 in a four-beat pattern. Continue with your partner, your neighbor, facing center and then with your back to the center.

CLAPPING SEQUENCE #9
A. This is the same as sequence #5 with the exception of adding a fifth beat to the sequence.
B. After the four basic patterns, add a fifth beat by using the hand that did not clap with the partner. Raise it above those that just clapped and let it clap your partner's hand.

Beginning on the third beat of this five-beat sequence, the left palm is up and is clapping horizontally the right palm of your partner, which is down. Then, on the fourth beat, the left hand of both people are clapping each other. On the fifth beat the left palm is clapping the left palm of the partner.

CLAPPING SEQUENCE #10
A. As before
B. As before
C. simple, as in sequence #1
D. The same as step B, clapping your own hands. This seems very easy and yet after all the preceeding sequences, is very awkward.

CLAPPING SEQUENCE #11
A. As before
B. As before
C. Repeat A (on thighs)
D. Repeat B (clapping)
E. Clap partner's hands, like step C in sequence #1

CLAPPING SEQUENCE #12
A. Repeat steps A, B, C and D IN #11
B. Begin the series of variations on step E of sequence #11 by having alternating palms up.

CLAPPING SEQUENCE #13
A. Use any of the above sequences, except sequences #5, 6, 7 or 8.
B. While doing the sequence with partners, the groups of two begin to slowly walk around the room.

CLAPPING SEQUENCE #14
A. Use any of the above sequences except #5, 6, 7, 8 or 13.
B. Have the partners jump rope as they do the sequence.

Students will invent their own sequences after this point. Over fifty sequences have been tested. Some are truly intricate and difficult. With an elementary class, do not spend too much time on this. They will learn it on their own and will teach it to their friends in play. Every week, present a new variation for them to integrate into their sequences.

SPEAKING IN MUSICAL TONGUES

For all ages

In the exercise, "Being the Musical Brain", the right brain and the left brain had a conversation. The right brain could not use any words to express itself. Sounds and symbols were used.

In this exercise, the right brain will have a language to use to express itself. But the language will be a kind of secular, improvised tongue. This kind of glossalalia is a part of every child's life. They make up languages and words and friends' names every day. They have imaginary friends and experiences that seem as real as their true experiences.

This exercise is in two parts: verbal babble and musical babble.

Begin by having the participants stand in a circle. Tell them that they are going to invent a new language. Have them give the leader some words.....the leader then invents translations for them. Examples:

participant	leader
piano	tigkleklinks
oyster	yukscheller
blue	rah
funny	heheha

Now begin to give members of the group words. Have them make up the translation. Here is a sample:

leader	participant
flower	pediepopop
ugly	snurg
apple	korunsch
knee	blula

The leader then begins to act out a short story and narrates it in this made up language. To play with the word sounds and their lengths is important. After the story is told, ask for a participant to translate it into English.

Request that some of the participants make up short stories and tell them to the group. Then have the group translate. Then have everyone choose a partner. Each of the partners has three minutes to talk in his own new language. Each is to tell his partner about the biggest and most difficult problem in life. The partner only listens with compassion, giving an occasional pat on the back, hug or a verbal sigh. Some participants may find this difficult. Suggest that they only use vowels sounds to begin, and add consonants gradually.

After this exercise, it is helpful to have an instumentarium of Orff instruments available. If not, use an ensemble of the following: a piano, a drum, a tambourine, resonator bells, any available metallophones, xylophones, and glockenspiels, recorders, triangles and finger cymbals. In place of speaking our new language, the answer will be played before it is translated. Have the participants ask a simple question:

"How many sandwiches did you have for lunch?"

The leader then answers on any instrument. Usually with one or two sounds.

"How do you feel today?"

The leader finds an instrument that has the timbre of a mood. Then the leader asks the participants what kind of mood that was.

Roles are reversed and the participants play the answers and interpret them. This evolves into instruments asking questions of other instruments and being translated by other groups of children. This is truly "questions and answers" on verbal and musical levels simultaneously. It is important to remember that there are no wrong answers. That music serves to express a valuable answer to a difficult and perhaps unanswerable question is the foremost purpose of this exercise. This is also an excellent method for introducing improvisation.

MUSICAL VISUALIZATIONS

Activity
For groups or individuals
All ages

Musical visualizations are produced through a series of active physical activities, deep relaxation, listening and visualization techniques. The preparation for these mental journeys and experiences is the same.

Preparation for visualization:

Spend eight to ten minutes in active physical movement to music such as "The Sabre Dance," "Flight of the Bumblebee," or Tomita's "Kosmos." The movement should be improvisational with no standard dance pattern. It is essential to visualization for the motor cortex to be activated as the first step.

Have the students then lie down on their backs with their eyes closed. A carpeted room is needed or a gym with proper mats. As their eyes are closed and their breathing becomes heavy, suggest to them that they are entering a period of active resting. They are not going to sleep, or daydream, but are awakening their brains as their bodies were similarly awakened. The brain is not going to be awakened by a variety of left-brain thoughts or uncentered discussions, but is to be awakened with clear inner vision and expanded ability to listen. Balance the breathing, allowing for slower and fuller breaths. If there is any tension in the body, exhale it. Inhale comfort, peace and clarity. This process should take three or four minutes. The suggestions made by the leader should be in softer, slower words than normal speech. There should never be any strain for the participants to hear. If there are many distracting sounds outside the room, suggest to the participants that they not pay attention to those sounds. but allow them just to pass through their ears and not hold on to them as a thought in the brain. "Relax the body and awaken the brain." "Inhale peace and comfort into the left part of the brain, exhale all busy thought from the left part of the brain." "Inhale a feeling of well being into the right part of the brain, exhale all anger or discomfort from the right part of the brain."

This is the preparation for all musical visualizations to follow:

Musical Visualization I

The House of Perfect Music

1. Begin with preparation.

2. Begin music: Side One, CHARIOTS OF FIRE by Vangeles (Polydor)

3. Suggestions given by the leader:

"In our state of awakened mind and relaxed body, we are going to approach the House of Perfect Music. It is a place where sound makes up the perfect structure of beauty, strength and peace all at one time. Visualize yourself as a very tiny being on one of your big toes. You are so small that you can travel in and out of the skin and bones of your body as you wish. Slowly dive into your toe and begin to observe what it is like being inside yourself with all the inner light needed to see the wonderful variety of colors and textures. Slowly travel through your foot and up your left leg, taking advantage of the scenery. Soon you will pass right under your knee cap and enter the thigh and the pelvic area. Continue through the center part of your body observing the left and right parts of the lungs and internal organs, remembering how different this part of your body is from the legs where you were just a few moments ago. Observe the rhythmic heart and all of its interesting networks and colors. Slowly enter into the neck and observe the curious passageways of the nerve centers, the air channels and the muscles and cartilage. Be careful not to get in the way of a gushing swallow. Continue into the head to the facial area and be aware of the wonderful sensations of taste. Spend a moment thinking of your whole body having the ability to taste just as your mouth can. Then think of the nose and how it can smell a variety of aromas. Invent one of your favorite smells for you to remember right now. Think of the skin on the outside of your face and how it can feel the sensations of the fresh ocean air, the mist of the ocean spray and the sunshine which is now shining on it. Continue into your eyes, even though they are closed, and observe them seeing the most interesting and beautiful things in the world; a horse galloping in a lush green meadow with the yellow flowers of spring in the background. Imagine a sunset from the highest mountain in Colorado with its magnificent orange, red and yellow rays of light. (Allow time up to a minute between each visualization.) Imagine a perfectly full moon with a background of shimmering planets and thousands of stars. Now envision yourself as this little being.....able to bring all of these wonderful feelings together; the smell of the fragrant air, the touch of the cool wind, the sight of a glorious sunset, and now add the taste of your favorite pie. You are nearly completely awake within your brain.

Enter your ears and listen deeply to the music which is being played. As you listen, continue to taste, feel, see and smell all the wonderful sensations.

Now enter your brain. To the left is your logical thinking mind, everything you know. Some parts of it are orderly and some parts are a little mixed up. To the right is your sound mind, full of ideas, inspiration, music and feeling that you cannot quite put into words. Honor these brains. Give them a sense of respect and well-being without any challenge or conversation. Suggest to both of them to awaken to a fuller ability. Tell each one about the other brain, what it is like and how it acts. Spend a moment introducing them to each other. Tell them that when they work together and understand each other, even though they are very different at times, they can produce the most wonderful and memorable experiences. (two minutes for these conversations, all held silently within)

(gently turn off the music and enter into silence)

Now that our brains, senses and bodies are very awake and aware of themselves, we are going to let them work with each other in creating the House of Perfect Music. Let the little person within begin to build your own House. Let every idea from every part of you make a contribution. Each piece of scenery and the surroundings of your house can been seen, felt and heard. Each piece of material, marble, wood, or whatever is best for you can be heard, if not as a musical sound, any other kind of sound. Every piece of furniture you put in every room can be heard. Listen carefully and take your time. It may take you a few minutes to prepare your house or it may suddenly just appear, all ready at one time. Just pay complete attention with your whole mind and body to what you are hearing. You may hear a familiar piece of music, or you may hear a variety of sounds, old and new. You may know some of the instruments you hear and some may be uninvented yet. Listen, deeply listen in the most awakened place you have ever been.

(wait about three minutes in silence while the visualization is taking place)

Now keep your House of Perfect Music clearly in front of your closed eyes and in front of your open ears. Take a photo of it with your mind so that it will never be forgotten. Its perfect state and perfect harmony exist now in a part of your mind which can be returned to whenever you need the inspiration and peace. That House of Perfect Music is yours. You may add some more to it, but nothing can take it away.

(quietly turn on music again)

Leave your two brains now. Slowly let your little being walk downwards through your body. Take time to observe it. (20 seconds) Come to the toes again and perch this little being on one of the toes. Remember the past experiences and begin to wiggle the toes and feet. Slowly stretch your feet and legs, then arms and whole body. Yawn, if you like, and slowly open your eyes to the room where you are. Just remain on your back for a moment, listening to the music and remember the House of Perfect Music.

Slowly sit up. Notice the colors of the room, the people in the room. Do you see it any differently? Now quietly find two people nearby, and in groups of three, tell each other about your experiences.

Share the experiences with the leader and compare visualizations. (This works well with most ages. Modify it to fit the needs of very small children.)

Musical Visualization II

Left Brain/Right Brain

> This exercise is a variant of the exercise given by Jean Houston in her book, *The Possible Human*. (J.P. Tarcher, Los Angeles, 1982)

1. Begin with preparation.

2. Begin music: A thirty-minute tape of simple, minor ostinati on a bass xylophone.

3. With your eyes closed, move all the relaxed awareness in your body up to your brain. Concentrate on your eyes; move them up to the top of your head, then let them move all the way down as if they were gazing at the feet. Repeat this slowly four or five times. Then move your eyes to the right, and then to the left. Repeat this four or five times. Then circle both eyes clockwise five times. Then very slowly move them counterclockwise five times. Slowly to the left, then down, then right and up. Now continue to circle clockwise and then counterclockwise with your concentration just on your right eye. Do this alternating motion five times. Then move your left eye clockwise, then counterclockwise four or five times alternately.

Relax your eyes for a minute and observe which eye was easiest to move in this manner. Now concentrate on both sides of your brain. Which one seems more accessible than the other?

Keeping your eyes closed and relaxed, imagine the images that will be suggested as vividly as possible. Don't strain as you do this:

On the left side of your brain imagine the number 1....

And on the right side the letter A....

On the left side the number 2....

And on the right side the letter B....

On the left side the number 3....

And on the right side the letter C....

On the left side the number 4....

And on the right side the letter D....

On the left the number 5....

On the right the letter E....

Continue with the numbers on the left and the letters on the right, going toward the number 26 and the letter Z. You don't have to actually reach 26 and Z. Just continue for a minute or so. If you get confused or lost, go back to the place where the letters and numbers were clearly together and begin again.

Rest for a minute, relaxing your attention as you do so. Now reverse the process you have just done, putting the letters on the left and the numbers on the right.

On the left imagine the letter A....
And on the right the number 1....
On the left the letter B....
And on the right the number 2....

Keep going toward the letter Z and the number 26.

Now stop and rest for a moment. Notice whether it was easier on one side of the brain or the other, whether numbers or letters were more clearly visualized.

(the leader should take a pause of five or six seconds between each of the suggestions below)

Continuing with your eyes closed, visualize the following:

On the left side of your brain is a river flowing in the mountains.
On the right side of the brain is a dry Egyptian desert.
Let go of the river on the left and replace it with a grove of fragrant orange trees.
Let go of the desert on the right and replace it with the sight and taste of a peppermint stick.
On the left is your mother.
On the right is a piece of chocolate cake.
On the left is a bulldozer.
On the right is a saxophone player playing "Twinkle Twinkle Little Star."
On the left is a newspaper.
On the right is an oyster.
On the left is the fire station in your neighborhood.
On the right is the moon.
On the left is a clown.

On the right is a marching band playing "Jesus Loves Me."

On the left is a tropical sandy beach.

On the right is a puppy.

On the left is your grandfather.

On the right is a strawberry ice cream sundae.

On the left is a piano.

On the right is a car driving in the fog.

On the left is your music teacher dressed as a pickle.

On the right is a red banana.

On the left is a phonograph playing "This Old Man."

On the right is the feeling of crawling over rough rocks.

On the left is the sound of a police car.

On the right is the feeling and taste of melted marshmallows.

On the left is the smell of tar.

On the right is the feeling and smell of glue stuck on the fingers.

On the left is the smell of apple juice.

On the right is the feeling of a cat licking your hand.

On the left is Pac Man.

On the right is the smell of your favorite meal being prepared.

Now on the left side of your brain, visualize and experience as fully as you can the
following scene: You are riding an elephant through a rainstorm at night carrying
two chickens under your right arm and a hamster in your left hand; you are chewing
bubble gum and listening to the news on your headphones.

On the right side of the brain you are skating in circles on green ice, wearing a mink
coat, humming "The Star Spangled Banner", chewing tobacco and looking at a full
moon in front of you and a rainbow above you.

On the left side of the brain you see triangles.

On the right side you see circles.

On the left side you see dozens of little boxes.

On the right side you see hundreds of marbles.

On the left side you see everyone's face in this room.

On the right side you see everyone's shoes in Dayton, Ohio.

On the left side you smell every fish in the world.

On the right side you smell every rose in the world.

On the left side you see every neuron and cell in your left brain.

On the right side you see every neuron and cell in your right brain.

On the left side you see the state of Georgia with all its trees, schools, people and peanuts.

On the right side you see every person in the world that is practicing music.

On the left side you see every basketball game that has ever been played.

On the right side you see every person in the world doing something kind and unexpected to another person.

On the left side you see yourself sharing something with a person you have never met.

On the right side you see someone whom you don't know giving you a gift.

On the left side you see yourself as the happiest you have ever been in your life.

On the right side you see a football stadium made of cottage cheese.

On the left side smell icicles.

On the right side taste a half drop of gasoline.

Now put a hummingbird on each side of your brain and then let each gently buzz over the opposite brain. Turn the hummingbirds into eagles and let them soar and loop throughout your brain, finally perching in a tree in the opposite brain from where they started.

Now put a hummingbird on the right and an eagle on the left and let them fly in their own manner to opposite sides of the brain.

Now let there be a calm horizon on both sides of the brain. Let it be gentle and quiet. You are feeling the beauty and peace of a sunset. You notice a quiet and lovely sailboat sailing in the calm sea. Notice which direction it comes from and where it is going.

Now envision a hippopotamus. See it, smell it, hear it and observe its environment on both sides of the brain. Let it dance for a moment to such special music only you will hear, then let it return to its natural activities. Let it continue to tell you a little story by its actions. (wait one minute)

Now imagine Santa Claus in his sleigh flying down in front of you in the sky. The heavens are full of a million stars and the sound of thousands of sleigh bells are everywhere. Santa is now going faster and faster, around and around and around, and faster and faster, beginning to spiral up and up and up and up, faster and faster and faster, it is going up and up and up right to the top of your head, then around and around and down and down to the chin, then faster and faster it goes up and up and then faster and faster it comes down and down right down to the chin and mouth where you swallow him and smile and forget all about it.

Gently go back to your left and right brains, sense them both at the same time. Imagine that your breath is allowing your brain to grow and expand, and when you exhale, it contracts and relaxes even more.

Now here is your opportunity to talk to your whole brain: for you to tell it anything you like, and for it to respond creatively in a way it has never done before. It has been activated with imagination. It doesn't challenge itself. It is itself and it is full. You can talk to it and listen to it. Go ahead!

Now with your whole brain and whole body, begin to stretch. Open your eyes and look at the room and people in it, remembering the visual experiences you have just had.

Find three people near you and form groups of four. Share the most interesting parts of this experience with each other. If you have drawing materials, draw the whole brain as you now feel it. If there are musical instruments, improvise on the impressions and compare them to other improvisations without visualization exercises.

Musical Visualization III

Listening with the Whole Body

adapted from Jean Houston's
techniques of synesthesis,
from *The Possible Human*.
(J.P. Tarcher, Los Angeles, 1982)

1. Begin with preparation

2. Begin music: Mahler's Symphony #2, Second Movement; Ravel's "Bolero", or Dukas' "The Sorcerer's Apprentice."

3. Suggestions given by the leader:
    "Picture your ears as you relax. Extend them in your imagination throughout your whole body. Think of yourself as one big ear with the ability to hear with any part of your body. (Your body does feel sound waves and is sensitive to sound, even though it does not hear as your ears do.) Let the sound of this music move in you, around, above you, below you. The sound is everywhere and you can hear it anywhere. See it, taste it, smell it, feel it and above all, hear it. You will not be disturbed for the whole piece of music. Turn all the sound into light and see it. Let the lightness and darkness come together with interesting contrast."

4. After this, let the participants paint or draw their reactions. Notice in an instrumental or choral rehearsal how such an activity at the beginning of a rehearsal relaxes the ensemble, improving musical attention and concentration.

TONING THE VOICE

No matter how many years we work with children's voices, there is always the challenge of the untuned voice. Surely there are keys within brain research that will assist us in the search for the tonal center of that ever-searching child. The psychological problems presented by a child with an untuned voice are multiple. The child may learn to "unenjoy" music because of the way the teacher and members of the class react to his singing. We realize that once a child is inhibited about a skill, whether physical or mental, it is far more difficult to change that pattern.

The periods of trial and error are of great importance to the tuning of a voice. Just as some children speak earlier than others, some voices tune earlier. How many times do we have to repeat the word "the" as a child before we are able to say it properly? Yet how many opportunities do we have to match tones with others correcting us? Children walk and speak at their own pace and I suggest that they do the same with vocal music. Children do not, however, have to take a class in "How to Utter" or "Self-propulsion." These skills develop out of the world in which children live and their desire to be a part of it.

Perhaps this is the process that the voice and the brain begin to find a tonal nature. Many children find their ear-to-voice relationship quite early and very naturally. Yet, many children do not discover it for environmental, neurological or physical reasons. When a nine-year-old is searching for a pitch, it may be because the child has no way of measuring the sound production itself.

Techniques of TONING the voice *before* tuning the voice, work very well to integrate the senses of vision, movement and music. Allowing the voice to discover naturally the pitch variance without any kind of matching motivation allows the voice to "get up and go." But where?

In the beginning, it does not matter. The sound of the voice must be free in its formative years to wander around and explore what possibilities it has. For the young voice to be focused on tunes and pitches with sufficient exploration and permission to do so can cause some frustration. Telling a child to go higher or lower, louder or softer, does not always help. Every child, every voice, has a different quality and texture. Finding ways to guide the voice to a correctly pitched and natural musical sound is the challenge.

There are many reasons why a child may not sing on pitch; ear and speech defects, breathing abnormalities from asthma to allergies, or psychological tension and stress. The child with little musical experience needs time to integrate a musical and tonal vocabulary. The younger child begins to sing and participate in multisensory musical experiences, the easier it is to adjust and tone the child's voice.

The exercises:

1. Spelling the child's name in sound.

   Have the children stand in a semi-circle so that they are aware of what each other is doing. Ask a child to spell her first name. For example, "Mary."

   Begin by stooping and pointing to the floor, making a low "who" sound and slowly stand up. As the hand and body rise, raise the pitch. Continue until the pitch is high and the hand is reaching above the head, then come at a slant down to the flor again, adjusting the pitch accordingly, the slant up again with the body and pitch and then come straight down to the floor. You have created the letter "M" in the air with the whole body stretching and stooping as well as pitch variation with the voice. The letters "T", "G", "H", "E", "L", "F" and "Z" all present the opportunity for the child to stabilize the sound on a constant pitch, whether it be with all the other children or just alone.

2. Symbols and drawings in sound

   As the children stand in a semi-circle, ask if anyone can draw the treble or G clef with their right hand and with sound as they have done in Toning Exercise 1. Then ask the class to do that also. Then make the same symbol with the non-dominant hand with the sounds. There is a wide variety of musical symbols as well as dollar signs, numbers and mathematical symbols that can be used for this exercise.

   Have children draw a tree, a house or a person with their hands in the air, sounding the variance of pitch as they do so.

   These exercises are devised to free the child of inhibition in varying pitches. Singing in tune comes at a later phase.

3. Searching for the hidden sounds

Have the children stand in a circle with the leader sitting in the middle of the circle. The children are mountains surrounding the leader, who calls out a sound. The mountains echo it back. (How often young children strain their voices, just by having to look straight up at a teacher.) This echo technique is then changed, to a sound hunt, much like an Easter egg hunt. The leader places a sound on the mountain and the mountain has to make that same sound to find it. This allows for all the other children to listen and it also gives permission to the child responding to the matching game to "look for" the sound. In other words, it is all right to search for the pitch, just as one would do in an Easter egg hunt. The children who match easily can assist the others in finding their sounds. By reversing this game, the very tuned.or the very untuned will both enjoy hiding a pitch on the leader to see if the leader can find it.

4. Faucets, knobs and levers

Toning the children's pitch by using imaginary faucets, knobs and levers is also helpful. The more they can see the examples of change as they see it on appliances, computers and instruments at home, the more effectively they will be able to sustain their pitches.

THE SOUND CAMERA

Activity for children

Have everyone in the class find a partner. Instructions are given before going into another room with many instruments.

"We are going to use our eyes like a camera. The shutter moves very quickly, so quickly that we hardly know that it has been opened at all. One of you will be the photographer and the other will be the camera. The photographer will lead his camera. The camera's eyes and lens are closed, not seeing a thing. When the photographer wants to take a photograph of something that is extremely beautiful or interesting, the camera is aimed and focused right on that subject.

The photographer tells the camera, "I'm ready to take a picture." At that time the photographer takes both hands of the camera and holds them to the camera's side. The hands are raised slightly, then "clicked" down to the side. The camera's eyes blink for only one second or less. Nothing is said. The photographer finds about 10 more photographs to take, slowly walking around looking for the best angle and view for the camera.

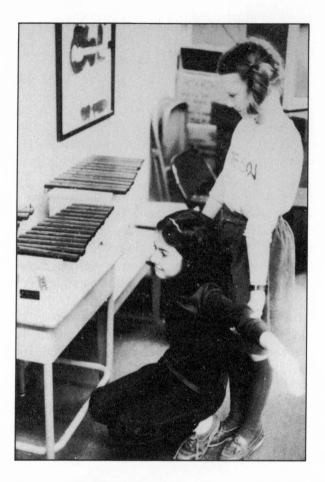

The camera must remember all ten photographs with as much detail and clear color as possible.

Then without any conversation and remembering that the only utterance is by the photographer just before taking a photo, the camera and the photographer change places and repeat the exercise."

There needs to be a great amount of space and a prepared variety of visual possibilities for the exercise.

After everyone has experienced being the camera, the photographer asks the students to sit in groups of four and tell each other what they saw. How different was it from regular vision? What was more interesting? What was clearer?

Then discuss these experiences as a class. How much do we see with our eyes open? How much more do we see when we have only a split second to observe it?

The exercises continue with the sound camera. Our ears become the lenses. With the eyes closed and the mind being very still, have the students imagine they are looking at a dark movie screen. There will be a flash of sound projected on the screen. There will be ten sound pictures. Each will be for only a second. Remember every detail as to what they see through the sound.

The exercise is best done when a prepared tape has been made with the ten examples. Space out each of the ten examples by approximately 30-second intervals of silence. It is better not to turn the recorder on and off during this exercise. Examples for the exercise may be done with live performances if possible or from a wide variety of examples such as the ones below:

1. The first six notes from a fast movement of a Bach Brandenburg Concerto.

2. The first four syllables of the "Toreador Song" from Carmen.

3. Two seconds from a very dissonant piece of electronic music.

4. The first three notes of "Taps" played on a bugle or trumpet.

5. Two seconds of an organ playing a beautiful hymn.

6. Two seconds of street noise.

7. One second of a soprano singing any one note on "ah".

8. Two seconds of three people whistling anything together.

9. The first theme of Beethoven's Ninth Symphony.

10. A burp.

After listening to the examples, ask the students to review what they have seen and heard. Bring the brief projections on to the screen again and with their eyes closed, hold up one finger at a time when they see their sound pictures again.

As this exercise is repeated every week, the teacher will observe much higher attention to and retention of the sounds. Children can make their own cassettes of these exercises and bring them to class for others to hear as an exercise.

In time, expand the amount of the sound photograph to three seconds, then five seconds, then a minute. The goal is to be completely attentive throughout a piece of music.

THE MUSICAL MAZE

Activity & Exercise
Individual or small group

Material needed:

— strong piece of white, smooth cardboard about 14" by 10" in size
— heavy duty string at least 8 feet in length.
— airplane glue
— two pieces of round felt, about the size of a dime

Draw on the board a maze like the one below:

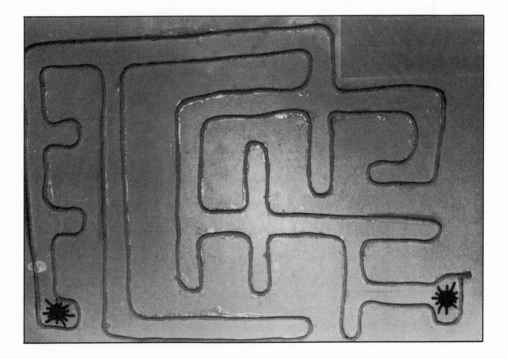

    The two parallel lines should be a least ⅝ inch apart so that the index finger of an adult or child can easily trace the paths between the strings without looking.

Using one continuous piece of string from the starting circle where there is a piece of round felt, glue the string over the lines, covering all parts of the string. After the glue has dried, cover the string with the glue again to attach it securely.

Steps for using the Musical Maze:

A.   Put the maze in front of the student. Have the student interpret the paths with pitch variations. The hands are not used in this first step. If the path is horizontal, the pitch should remain constant. If it moves upward or downward, the pitch should vary accordingly. There is no tonal center, nor is there any scale as to the amount of variation in the pitch. The purpose is to allow the young student the opportunity to tone his voice at different pitches.

B.   As the student closes his eyes, place the index finger of the dominant hand onto one of the felt circles. The goal is to reach the other felt circle. As the finger begins to search through the maze, the student also sings as the finger moves. The pitches should vary according to the direction of the hand.

C.   Repeat step B with the index finger of the non-dominant hand.

D.   As the eyes remain closed, place the dominant index finger at the felt pad at the finishing point of the maze and have the student trace the route in sound and touch in retrograde to the beginning point.

E.   Repeat step D with the non-dominant hand.

F.   Repeat step B with the board upside down.

G.   Repeat step C with the board upside down.

H.   Repeat step D with the board upside down.

I.   Repeat step E with the board upside down.

J.   Turn the board around, facing away from the student, so that the board is facing the class. Use steps B, C, D, E, F, G, H, & I.

The steps above are far too many for one sitting or class. With children who are developing a sense of pitch, pay close attention to their response as the dominant and non-dominant hands are used. The maze may also be traced with other fingers, the knuckles or the backs of the hands.

Some mazes may be drawn over a large staff with the horizontal paths in the spaces or on the lines. This is to be used with the eyes open as a part of music reading. This exercise is most helpful for older students who have pitch problems.

THE DEVIL'S TUNING FORK

Brain Game

Show the class an enlarged copy of the drawing below. Having already presented the information concerning how tuning forks work and why they are used, show it to class for thirty seconds; then ask them to draw it themselves and explain how it works.

Repeat this twice more, to see how the visual and verbal definitions improve.

THE LEGATO JUMP ROPE

Group Exercise
for children

In choral singing, the need for relaxed, upright posture is essential. Our skilled directors bring forth proper systems of sound production through breath support and proper vowel sounds. This exercise uses both the physical body and the use of imagery for relaxing the child's body.

1. Begin on the playground with eight or ten children to each long jump rope. Have two children turn the rope. Begin with some of their familiar chanting games, such as "3-6-9" in this chapter. Then begin to have all the children in each group begin to sing a familiar legato and somewhat slow song such as "Silent Night" or the themes of the Pachebel "Canon" on the text of "Alleluia".

2. Have all the children imagine the smoothest vocal line whether they are jumping or not.

3. Then have each child jump six times. The next time it is their turn, jump five times. Then four, three and two.

4. Then when back in the choir room, have them imagine themselves just beginning to run into the spinning rope. There is deep breath and usually one that is naturally supported. Then concentrate on the motion of jumping *without* moving the body at all. This is kinesthetic visualization.

5. Their bodies should be relaxed upward with no tension in their shoulders. The legato songs or warm-ups can then be sung with the imagery of the motor cortex in action.

Older choirs may find a variation in this exercise by dancing rather than jumping rope. By putting a dance beat with an electronic rhythm section while the choir members are vocalizing, you will often notice tensions held within the body released to free the vocal sound.

119

KINSESTHETIC TECHNIQUES FOR ORFF-SCHULWERK

Exercise & Activity
Individual or Group Activity
All Ages

These exercises are designed to integrate visualization and motor skills for greater memory and facility in musical performance. Once the basic techniques are learned, the skills can be applied to any instrument. Please review the introductory comments about kinesthetic learning in chapter five before using these exercises.

1. Kinesthetic hands

Begin with a very simple sequence of *patschen* (slapping palms on lap) and clapping:

clap:

patsch:

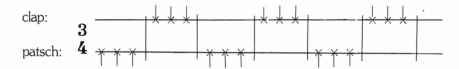

This is easily learned through immediate imitation. Concentration should begin on the clapping. As the students are clapping, ask them to be aware of the feeling of clapping. Ask them to pay attention to their hands as they are lifted from their laps for the clapping. Ask them to pay attention to how far the hands separate between the claps and to notice if the distance is always the same. Concentrate on the thumbs of the hands: what sensations are being experienced? Ask the students to concentrate on one finger at a time as the patschen and clapping are taking place. Be aware of the wrists, elbows and shoulders as the clapping is being done.

With the same rhythmic sequence, ask the students to continue the same body actions without the hands coming together on the claps. This is called the quiet clap. The hands make the same motion, but stop just an inch before making the percussive contact. Ask the student to be aware of the muscles in his hands, arms and shoulders as this quiet clap is made. Alternate between the actual clapping and the quiet clapping and ask the students to observe the difference in their hands. Continue to do this with the eyes closed.

Now ask the students to rest their hands on their laps, close their eyes and just imagine the feeling of clapping their hands. Using their imagination and muscle memory, ask them to clap ten times with their invisible hands. Then begin the clapping sequence below:

imagined clap:

quiet clap:

normal clap:

patsch:

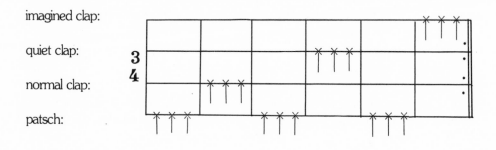

IT IS ESSENTIAL TO THIS EXERCISE that the last measure with the three imagined claps is not thought of as RESTING. The same mental process for normal clapping and quiet clapping must continue during the imaginary clapping. This is the basis for all kinesthetic.exercises. The memory of movement in the mind and the mind's ability to repeat it without the physical motion is what is meant by kinesthetic motion at this stage.

Remember the last time you were a front seat passenger with a driver who was not a careful driver? Did you put on the brakes? Or did you just want to? Did your kinesthetic right foot use the brakes as you were trying not to show the driver how uncomfortable you were? This kinesthetic memory is similar.

Use dozens of similar rhythmic patterns. Add snapping as another step. Use sequences in 5/4 and 7/4 time. These are far better brain builders because they do not fit into a habitual physical pattern. Three patchen and two claps work very effectively.

2. Kinesthetic Mallet Instruments

    The same technique used in exercise #1 is to be used with bar instruments as shown in the photographs.

    Use two mallets for a position of the perfect fifth on a xylophone. Play a series of four half notes on this interval, thus building the skill into the student. If there is only one instrument in a classroom, the other students can learn the skill by holding rhythm sticks or even pencils and using their laps as the xylophone bars.

    It is helpful to use a little different vocabulary in this exercise. "Bars," "air" and "mind" work very effectively in what we were calling "normal clap," "quiet clap" and "imagined clap" in the previous exercise.

    There are two important aspects in working with this exercise. It builds the kines-thetic ability to integrate the skill into a memory pattern that lasts longer. More important is the ability for all students to learn an ostinato pattern before approaching the instrument for the trial and error sequence. Many complicated patterns can be easily taught to a full class with this technique.

3. Kinesthetic Jumping

    To overcome the possibility of using the kinesthetic actions as a resting time for the mind or body, the class may need to put it into action in a non-musical exercise.

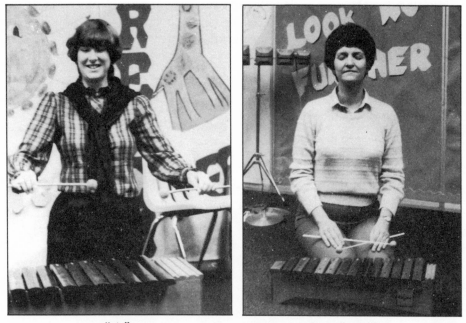

"air"   "mind"

"bars"

Have the class stand in a circle and review the simple game of "Mother, May I?" The kinesthetic or imaginary body will be called the "K body." The physical body will be called the "P body." A sequence like the following may be used:

P body, two steps forward.
P body, two steps back.
P body, one step to the right.
P body, one step to the left.
K body, one step forward.
K body, one step back.
P body, one step to the left.
P body, one step to the right.
K body, one step to the left.
K body, one step to the right.
P body, one step back.
K body, one step forward.
P body, one step forward.
K body, one step back.

Now at the same time, have the P body jump back one step and the K body jump forward one step.

Now have the P body jump forward a step and the K body jump back a step. Do this five times.

Now at the same time, have the P body jump forward one step and the K body jump back one step.

Now have the P body jump back one step and the K body jump forward a step. Do this five times.

Have the P body jump to the right and the K body jump to the left.

Have the P body jump to the left and the K body jump to the right.

Have the P body jump to the left again and the K body jump to the right again.

Then have the P body jump to the right and the K body jump to the left.

4. Kinesthetic movements

This group of exercises allows endless variations on kinesthetic skills and visualization. It is suggested that the physical movements in Chart A be done as an activity over a period of time so that the students are familiar with the variety of combinations before introducting it kinesthetically. Some of the combinations are impossible and imply a humorous play movement. "With your *hips*, begin to *sink* very *dreamily* toward *the window*."

In Chart B, use the visualizations for stimulating the use of sound in a variety of situations. "Imagine the sound of *an icecube singing*." "Imagine the sound of a *turtle sneezing*."

This exercise is difficult if the participants have not developed visualization techniques. Using a variety of instruments, especially a synthesizer, is quite helpful. The goal is to expand the possible vocabulary of sounds.

Chart A

COMBINATIONS OF MOVEMENTS

"With your....	begin to....	very....	toward....
head	walk	slowly	the sky
eyes	run	quickly	the earth
tongue	spin	lightly	the nearest tree
chin	crawl	heavily	the hall
shoulders	gallop	freely	windows
elbows	leap	strongly	your right
hands	skip	quietly	your left
fingers	slide	loudly	the piano
chest	hop (1 foot)	gracefully	me
hips	jump (2 feet)	awkwardly	Idaho
knees	stretch	funnily	the moon
legs	shrink	sleepily	the drums
feet	melt	consciously	your house
toes	tilt	dreamily	your feet
whole body	grow	excitedly	your stomach
imaginary body	rise	silently	your center
center	fall	sustained	your left brain
tummy	swing	inhibitedly	your right brain
	creep	beautifully	the music
	slither	randomly	the color blue
	vibrate	rigidly	the color red
	prance	frigidly	nowhere
	bounce		everywhere
	soar		silence
	fly		noise
	shake		your best friend
	roll		your fifth best friend
	drip		your favorite smell
	float		your favorite book
	coil up		
	expand		
	glide		
	shiver		
	tingle		
	tumble		
	wobble		
	sink		
	freeze		
	advance		
	retreat		
	twist		
	curve		
	clap		
	feel		
	touch		

Chart B

COMBINATIONS OF INNER SIGHTS AND SOUNDS

"Imagine the sound of........   ....

a snowflake	singing
an icecube	whistling
a popsicle	playing a banjo
a breeze	humming
a candle flame	laughing
a cave	calling home
a rainbow	screaming
an earthquake	speaking
a volcano	whispering
a hurricane	chewing gum
a tornado	crying
a drop of rain	eating donuts
a river	sneezing
a ray of light	sleeping
a grain of sand	dreaming
an ocean	breathing
a friend	dancing
a teacher	shouting
a Frenchman	loving
a Chinaman	snoring
a cricket	screeching
a fish	
a dog	
a cat	
a chicken	
a cow	
a horse	
a snake	
a turtle	
a whale	

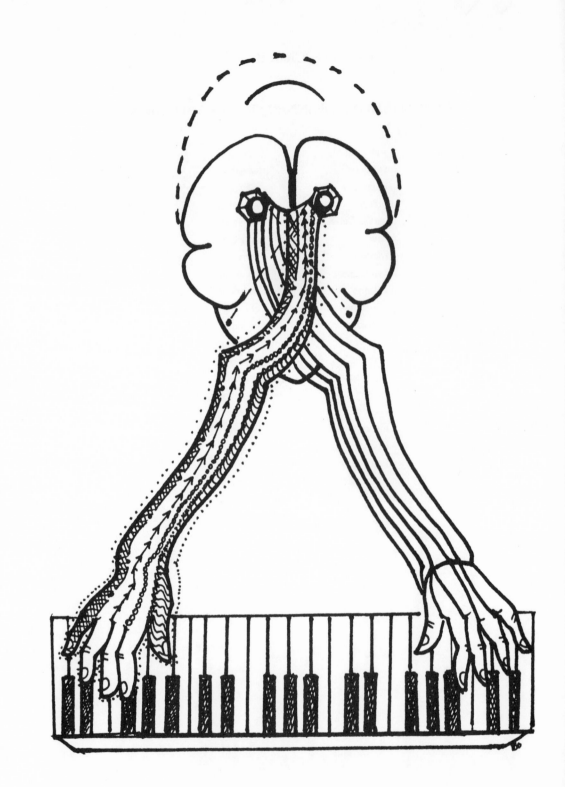

MENTAL KEYBOARDS

Exercise
Mental Keyboards

1. Use a one-or two-octave scale or a thematic phrase from the Bach Two-part Inventions. Have the student play it as written in the right hand. Then have the student with eyes closed repeat it in the mind without moving the fingers.
2. Repeat it with the fingers on the piano bench, then look at the music. Play it again with the music.
3. If the phrase is memorized, go on to the next step. If not, repeat the ones above.
4. Play the initial phrase or scale with the left hand making the proper adjustments for satisfactory fingering. Then repeat steps 1, 2, and three.
5. Play the phrase with both hands together on the keyboard, then on the imagined keyboard without any physical movement, then on the piano bench. Repeat if necessary.
6. Cross the hands, left over right, to play the phrases again on the keyboard, then on the imagined keyboard, then on the piano bench.
7. Scale work can then be done with endless variations in rhythm.
8. A more advanced variation is done with the eyes closed. The student only hears the phrase and repeats it without reading music.
9. Imagine a keyboard for the feet. Not an organ pedalboard, but a keyboard slightly larger than the regular keyboard. As you are learning the melody of a piece, for instance the theme from Bach's d minor two-part Invention:

Now with the knowledge of the fingering from playing it with your right hand, use the same fingering and play it with your right foot's toes. Difficult and impossible with the physical toes, but facility with the imagined toes is simpler. Imagine it four or five times with the right foot, then begin to try it with the left foot's toes. Imagine it with the toes of that foot; then put both feet together.

This exercise is most effective with phrase and scales that are difficult for the student. When it is transposed through the perception of the senses to another part of the body, the information is reinforced in the hands where it is needed for performance.

THE INTERESTING BORING GAME

Brain game
All ages

List menial tasks which students do not like to do but which are part of their life. (washing dishes, cleaning their room, delivering the papers, vacuum cleaning, making beds, mowing the lawn or sitting in a boring class) Have some of the students mime the activity in a type of charade game as the class guesses what they are going. Begin to improvise rhythmic motion to the activity. What songs represent just the opposite of the activity? Sing them while the activity is being performed.

Goal: to keep the mind awake during menial and non-interesting tasks through music.

UNDER THE SPELL OF MUSIC

Brain game
All ages

Play a variety of stimulating music and have the students write their name with their right hand on a piece of paper if they are right-handed, then ask them to write their name with the opposite hand. Then ask them to stand and draw their name with the right arm wide in the air, then repeat with the left arm. Have them spell their name with their nose, then the tongue, then the left ear, then the right ear and then the whole head. Have them spell their names with the right foot, then the left foot, then the right shoulder and then the left one. Write the names with the left hip and then the right hip, then with their stomach. Then have them spell their name on the floor as they move their body around the room.

Choose a partner and communicate simple words with different parts of the body. Spell Bach, Beethoven or Handel with the elbow, for example. See if the partner can read what is being spelled.

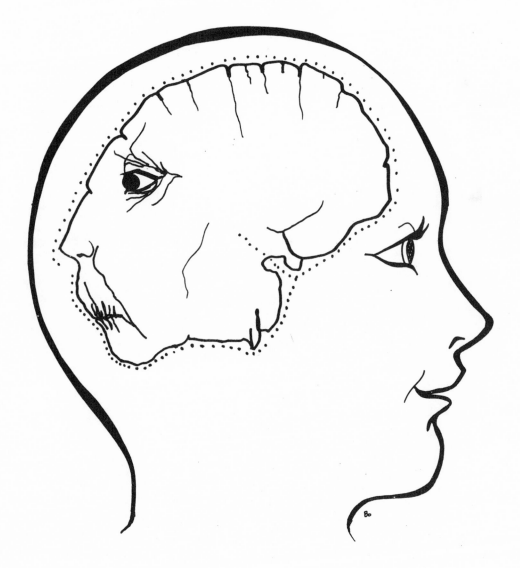

APPENDIX I

This interview does not deal with music as an independent study, but as part of an integrated system of arts for holistic education as demonstrated in the Mead School in Byram, Connecticut. For further information, refer to an extensive article on the Mead School in the **Saturday Review**, *September 3, 1977, pages 11 - 16.*

Matters of Consequence

Dr. Elaine de Beauport
in dialogue with Jane Prettyman

Speaking of the Rockefeller Report, Dr. Jean Houston said. "They're talking about 'arts in education.' We're talking about the developing human capacities and the arts' role in that."

The difference is important and the task of finding models to illustrate her point is not easy, but we can take heart in a few examples which have managed to thrive in our midst. One such is the Mead School for Human Development in Byram, Connecticut, for children ages 3 through 12. Founded in 1969 and until 1978 directed by Elaine de Beauport, this haven for the nurturing of the whole child grew from the premise that "art, music and man's spirit will not be secondary to other subjects."

Because of the rich experiential and multi-modal nature of the arts, they are primary at Mead. The links between the arts and other more sequential learning are evident in the repeated motifs of painting, weaving, music or body movment which provide more accessible patterning for the learning of language and math. The child has at hand the widest variety of modes and materials to make connections according to his or her particular strengths. Inherent in art process is the continuing experience of being inquisitive, experimental, forming hypotheses and working with trial and error; these qualities are developed and heightened for active application in the sciences and humanities. Not to be forgotten is an additional value: motivation. In the process of creating their own symbols and succeeding in their own projects, the children gain confidence in the fact that they "can do," and will move more willingly to respond to given forms and procedures in other subjects.

In terms of organization, the keys to Mead are an educational program worked out in negotiations between student, teacher and parent: a "two-teacher" system; and a complex educational environment wherein "classrooms" are transformed into highly structured learning areas.

Underlying everything at Mead is respect for the individual child and encouragement of the child's trust in his or her individual talents. Growth occurs in multiplying and integrating strengths and enabling the child to ask for help wherever it is needed.

Each center (language, math, art, music, humanities, environment and body) contains areas for group and individual activity, as well as a choice of sequential and non-sequential modes of learning. In tandem with this curriculum system, a "homecenter" counselor moves with the child through the day to solve learning and human problems as they arise in the context of their reality. Mead is structured to provide for the complexity of the cognitive process in curriculum while attending to the sensitivity of the developing human being.

Per SAT scores, the average of all age groups is on or above grade level in every subject. More significantly, children who were below grade level in language or math in the first three years were on or above level by their fifth or sixth year. These same students were outstanding in arts in primary years and continued to be so later. Meanwhile they developed as capable students in both the sequential mode required by testing and the associational mode required by the strengths of their individual dispositions.

The arts provide an entryway into the world least impeded by cultural expectations. For many, they are a crucial first step in an act of creation that continues through life and profession, as we do well what we know how to do, no matter how we know it.

Mead resonates with what "art" means. It's in the air, in the movement, the making of choices, in the expression of the inner being in the outer form of a language of one's own. The space itself is an artform of imaginative structuring for a honeycomb of possibilities. Imagine - in your adult state - becoming aware as you walk toward a park bench that you have definite feelings about where on the bench you will want to sit down. Do you opt for a spot near the armrest or do you land in the open center? The simplest of outer structures offers options for the expression of one's inner modality. Variation of structure allows for organic integration and the free flow of energy, as we see in cellular organization. Indeed, though we have no hard evidence yet, it may be that a flexible physical environment has beneficial effects upon older parts of the brain - the limbic system and reptilian complex -which, when free of blocked energy, might be less likely to disrupt the functioning of the neo-cortical hemispheres. Whether or not this is true, the good results in terms of cognitive development at Mead emerge from an atmostphere which allows the growing child to be with others or to be alone, to be supported or to be expansive. To be and to become.

What follows is a conversation with the person who began the process of allowing Mead to happen.

— Jane Prettyman

JP: What have been some of the attitudes that have held us back from understanding how vital a role the arts play in education?

EdB: As adults we go to museums to see art, magazines write about art, but our view of art is passive. We've become recipients of art, just as we're recipients of science, history and everything else. There's no process, no interaction, no engagement, no movement. If you say "art" to an adult, it implies the feeling of a set-apart *thing*, an object -which is totally different from the ancient point of view wherein art was craft, a way of dealing with one's environment. Art was how you found your way.

I don't think we can begin to talk about "art in education" until we ask what the adult thinks of when you say "art in education." As long as he sees the sculpture or the painting from the position of receiver, he will think, "Well, of course we should have art in schools for our children; of course they must learn *about* art." But he will not see that for some people art is their major mode of engaging in the world. If you say *this* to him, he will say, "Oh, you mean the artist." It's not just the artist. It may be anyone who has a dominant sensory or "feeling" way of doing things, who has right-hemisphere strengths. How many people learn this way, we don't know, but we *do* know how many fail to learn the sequential way. And how many with sequential strengths never develop their capactiies in the right hemisphere? By consigning the option of art process to the shelf of "thing," everybody loses.

Whether it's "the arts *in* education" or "the arts *and* education" we still have the implication of the "the arts" meaning dance, poetry, painting, sculpture, and "education," meaning doing your work in history, science, English or math - and there's the split. It's not integrated. The leap over - or the leap back - has to be made.

Perhaps it is the word "art" which separates us. We need to look at the process of opening and closing. When the mathematician sees a form, he comes to closure around a formula or a solution. It has an aspect of beauty because it relates, it's synthesized, it's complete. His coming to closure with numbers is very special and holds beauty for him, just as a drawing is beautiful in coming to closure with pastels. This is one way across all our separations. When the mathematician or the historian or the scientist comes to that moment of "Aha!" he comes to a closure similar to the experience of the artist. We go to the museum and see the closure which is hanging on the wall and we call the guy who made the thing an artist, and we call the guy who can put the plumbing together in our kitchen a plumber. I would say the capacity he has to put those pipes together quickly, effectively and succinctly makes him an artist with pipes. The day we call the mathematician, the historian - or the plumber - an artist, we will have opened a new dimension.

Our schools need to allow for expansive exploration, a lot of experiential digging, making mistakes, mucking around, crosses, leaps - all to serve as a base for deeper learning. Whether the closure is predominantly sequential or predominantly associational will depend on the natural strengths of the individual. *First* we must pay attention to that deep exploratory, experiential quality we've closed right out of our schools. It was long ago closed out of society which is why you don't find it in schools anymore.

JP: How does the receiver/creator split prove harmful in the learning process itself?

EdB: If all our teaching is done in verbal or number symbols - that is, you never give me materials with which to work; what you give me instead is the alphabet and you teach me numbers and the sequential procedures - then I have to learn what you teach me and, through testing, give it all back in the mode that you taught me. This is terrific if my procedural strength happens to be sequential - *and* if I'm willing to accept your symbols instead of creating my own. I sit down and shut up and receive your symbols peacefully and we've got a good thing going. The problem is this is *all* that's going in schools. If, on the other hand, I should have interrelational, associational, spatial capacities with strength in my right hemisphere, the fact that you want me only to do a procedure that I don't think is interesting really bugs me. At eight I can create a painting of a clown but you want me to write "The clown is here," your mental task is not as exciting as my mental activity. It is moronic compared to my mental activity. Plus, you not only want me to use a procedure that is not my strength: you don't even want to see the symbols I create. I can make many complex sounds with my voice which are symbolic, as is my form on a skateboard, and when I paint, that is symbolic too. But you don't want to honor the symbols that emerge from my stronger side. You won't let me use my brain.

So therein, I believe, lies a destructive split right at the beginning of education.

I could learn more if you would let me have the experiential in language and math. What's happening with an associational mind is I get to play with art materials and manipulatives, I get to touch them and feel them and make associations rather than just receive. I can enter into language or mathematics actively, I can get into the action of it, the coming to grips, to closure, the making it mine and the turning around of the form. This is very different from the passive receptive "You give me the form, I absorb it..."

JP: What does this mean for teachers, or, as you have called them, "to-eachers"?

EdB: It means they must completely relearn - re-*member* - their occupation. We learned to be teachers via left-hemisphere or sequential modes - that's *how* we succeeded. We pass on knowledge to others via the same sequential mode. It doesn't do any good to *tell* me that I have to understand what experiential or associational modes are. If I never use them I can't make it possible for children to use them. Any teacher who walks into his classroom without planning his lesson to provide for both forms of learning will disadvantage all the children in front of him in one way or another. To really enhance learning, the math teacher, the science teacher, the history teacher, the English teacher needs to have the new learning in right-hemisphere modes. Re-training programs must be designed to enable the teacher to experience these modes himself so that the lesson plans and the subtleties of helping children will reflect them.

JP: What about money for this re-training?

EdB: If you checked the national statistics for the number of dollars being spent on remedial education, you'd be shocked. One idea may be to use some of *those* funds. It takes more money to train a remedial specialist, to set up separate remedial sections in schools...

JP:...which still run along sequential lines...

EdB: Yes, it's still the same approach broken down for better assimilation as sequential learning. Whereas if we approached the so-called "problem learner" with respect for the child's particular cognitive strengths, we might not have such a need for remediation.

We're not very daring in education. If you trace the history, you'll see we solve problems by just adding another program. We add home economics, we add art, we add hot lunches, we add "learning disabilities" - it's a long list of additions. That's the problem. Nobody wants to go in and restructure and challengingly put themselves on the line. Money is not the point. The point is there is not enough courage.

JP: We're looking for a cognitive ecology, for integration...the links...

EdB: When we explore the links, we will better understand children who are now "failures." We will find openings to active as well as receptive learning. We will find the means to make expansive, multi-capacity knowing a reality. The links between the arts and learning lead us across to the other half of the brain; they let us use the whole brain. They also could lead us to a more balanced way of structuring education and a new understanding of cognition. To the present definition that requires the acceptance of forms, we would add the creation of forms. To the acceptance of procedures, we would add the creation of procedures. Knowing would include not only the use of symbols agreed upon throughout ages, as in language and math, but also the creation of symbols in art, music and physical performance. Acceptance and creation would be equal partners in the cognitive process.

JP: How did we get so one-sided?

EdB: We've learned how to organize the passive but we haven't yet learned how to organize the active. We've had the attitude of "What I gotta do is get you all educated" -give the knowledge I have. Then comes the little problem of "How come you don't get it?" Well, I guess either I'm not teaching you or you're dumb - and more likely it's that latter if I'm the teacher in power. Even if I'm the most humble teacher in the world, it's set up that way.

We make judgments not in terms of the characteristics of the human being but in terms of processing information which, through the long hard struggle of history, seemed to be knowledge that could be helpful to us. I'm not knocking that knowledge - what we have succeeded in is in many ways very beautiful. The issue is that in all the Golden Ages of high civilizations, that which represents knowledge, came from tremendous searching, experiencing, and intermingling of inner and outer. To take that and put that *upon* the human being is not going to work. We need to return to the experiential program - and art is one avenue.

I think we've simply never come to a deep valuing of human life. We have to find a whole new outlook on the actual physical existence of the human being. How in God's name we ever lost the human being is the deepest mystery to me. Perhaps it was a need for survival, or greed for "more." Perhaps we never knew we lost it. We've created large well-meaning systems to try to share our knowledge, believing we are in service of "humanity." We may be in service of the majority of humanity but there's a serious question as to whether that's the same as being in service to human life.

JP: The physical and athletic are other avenues of evocation in human development. For example, refining this, how do individual sports differ in dynamics from team sports?

EdB: If you are alone as you would be in swimming, golf, skateboarding, tennis, or skiing, you have time to allow response and development from within yourself. To enable yourself to relate with the distance and the hill and the ski - the whole thing is associational. If you're on a team, team-wise the action is coming at you very fast and close. There's not as much time or space in team situations for that inner response. For younger kids it's really important that there are individual sports available first or at least parallel with team sports. Some kids with high visual capacity and right-hemisphere capacities may be afraid of the team. Some have such a hypersensitivity and alertness that if they're put into a kick-ball game there may be too much power coming too fast. As the individual player develops and becomes stronger, then his heightened perception should make him an outstanding team player later.

Individual sports have suffered the same status problem as the arts in terms of recognition in schools. But they play an important role in overall development. If my son had gone through the regular school system he would have been a B-plus verbal student because he has the usual left-hemisphere sequential strengths. At Mead he got the art which kept open the right-hemisphere, the inner, the capacity to express and relate creatively with outer form. He went on to Whitby and picked up the guitar which became a love. So he had music. He played soccer as a goalie which is in its way an individual and creative position. Then he moved on to basketball as a center. So the right hemisphere was nurtured first by art, then by music and now by physical. He's an outstanding athlete now, I think because of the art and music - and because the physical was allowed a peaceful development.

The artist and the athlete, from the point of view of the brain, are not opponents. Why are they so in education and society? Could we not move to an understanding of *all* the arts - the visual, musical and physical?

JP: There were moments when I played tennis when I felt loose and completely at ease with my body moving in synchrony with the ball, as if I were part of another dimension of knowing...

EdB: You were. You were in relationship with dimension. This is at the heart of it all. This is what our understanding of the hologram brings us. It means connecting and linking. This takes us back to the complexity of the child and allowing the links to happen, allowing him to experience and learn the links whether it's with paint or with numbers. To turn the whole learning process topsy-turvy and send it down a fast-moving educational system is not respecting the complexities of knowledge. It can only be called "knowledge" with quotes around it, a kind of packaged thing we're going to give to the kids. But the knowing has been disregarded, the linking...

JP: ...the grace...

EdB: ...allowing the child to be graceful in his movement and discovery, to experience moving the "C" around to "AT" to make "CAT," moving geometric forms together in patterns, moving sounds into song...

JP: How can we acknowledge this process of invention?

EdB: Even if we have ten hours of the arts, it still won't make a hoot of difference because the status in schools works so that you only graduate if you have passing grades in the sequential modes. If you get an "A" in art, music, or gym, you don't get a diploma. The number of hours is not where the issue lies. The gut of the issue lies in status. Perhaps we should have a Stanford Creation or Invention Test as well as the Stanford Achievement Test to make clear that we value creation as much as the acquisition of verbal and mathematical skills.

JP: We have a great deal of work to do. How do we regain the balance?

JP: We have a great deal of work to do. How do we regain the balance?

EdB: We have to correct our excesses in order to go forward. We've lost our sensitivity. We've been educated in an impersonal world and it will take a lot of work on the personal human level to regain our sensitivity to what it means to harm a child. Why don't we see the hurt? Can we even feel it within ourselves? We have been so educated in the non-personal, in the making of systems, in largeness, and in outer observation. Naturally we discovered some of the marvelous complexities of the outer world, but when we lost our capacity to judge when those outer complexities would blow us up, we slipped a few discs...One by one we must pick them up - the smallest bits of creation, the tiniest molecule, in a plant or inside ourselves. New dimensions of observation are awaiting us.

We've been making do with the human condition the way it is. As long as we are turning out people who can "function" in society, we don't question the value of the "knowledge" we're imparting - or the fact that in that "burning out" process we are leaving behind a percentage of very creative individuals. We measure progress by our accomplishments, but nobody ever looked at them and said, hey, you know these accomplishments might be very limited. We always looked at knowledge as sacred because it got us this far. What may we have been missing?

JP: My brother suffered a great deal in school. He was classified retarded, and was a lefty who was forced to write right-handed. He was given all sorts of tests to explain his "inability to learn." Finally he was sent to a special school where they let him draw and build things, just to keep him quiet. No attempt was made to translate the symbols from the art process to the disciplines in which he was tested. He missed several grades, but drew like mad all over his notebooks. Somehow he survived and is living in Paris writing poetry and short stories. But he had no help in finding his way. I was lucky. I got along with tennis. That was my inner/outer experience, my means of survival. I fared better than he, too, because I had acknowledgement as a champion.

EdB: If in school your brother could have been a poetry champion or an art champion as you were a tennis champion, he might not have been harmed. With the kids at Mead, it *happened.* And it only happened because all we were trying to do at Mead was say that art, music and man's spirit will not be secondary to other subjects. That was our opening statement. So we created a number of options and centers which were all equal in terms of the child's being able to choose. I didn't know what it meant then. It's only in looking back that I can see what it meant to those who would have been harmed. They got their acknowledgment in the art center, the music center, in individual sports, while the sequential work could be down-played during those sensitive early years. *Then* the teacher could engage the kid and say "OK, that's terrific, now why don't you go over and do your reading." The teacher was able to engage the child in a real way, in a person-to-person way because she had first acknowledged the child's strength.

JP: Can you elaborate on structuring and the importance of materials?

EdB: The progressive schools took all structure away in the belief that the child would blossom. I don't believe that. There's a gestalt world there and the child enters into that gestalt. Adults must provide as many varied structures in as wide a range as practical to facilitate the awakening interaction of inner and outer, to educate as much as is humanly possible. Learning centers must be arranged to operate on both individual and group levels. It all has to be thought out very carefully to allow the child the greatest flexibility within the structures.

In the art center there is the greatest array of materials for the child to express what's going on inside him. He can't tell you because he doesn't yet have the richness of a symbolic language system. I didn't know this kind of art was going to be created. I really didn't have a clue. I only had the clue that if you don't have a lot of words at that age, you better use anything you can get - and at that age anything you can get happens to be art.

JP: At Mead, the children may work side by side, exchanging information...

EdB: It's friendship, it's social. The energy is unleashed, stimulated. The dance is strengthened. And on the deeper feeling level, the bodies are there for an interchange of excitement, of celebration.

JP: How do the kids interrelate about art?

EdB: When a child walks out with his painting, the other kids say, "Oh, wow, let me see, I want to see." It's an object that enables feedback. There's no negative grudging. It's not a comparison. While one kid did a painting and gets to take it home, another did his weaving, and another has his sculpture he gets to take home. The "getting to take home" is very special. It's not "We will all collect our papers" at the end of class, and the effort disappears. It's "I finished my sculpture today" and the culmination of energy is retained. The kids and the teachers and the parents can then have the *experience* of reflecting on this created object that arrives in space in front of them with its own marvelous tangibility.

JP: Can you suggest in summary a better way for us to look at education today?

EdB: Learning is so much more powerful than teaching. If you unleash the energy of the human organism with its capacity to discover and relate, you have a dynamic vitality. In education we have a big body trying to teach a little body. But their big body can't get into the little body. And it can't know what 30 or even one little body really knows. The big body can't get *in* but the kid can get *out*. You can never get as close to the "best method" of teaching as the kid can get to learning. The interface of teacher and student needs to be structured in the learning environment so that the big *and* the little bodies can be supportive and can facilitate, encounter, challenge, love, fight, midwife - but never stop the energy of learning. The energy of the child goes out and engages in the environment, in the materials and with the teacher. It's our adult job to build the kind of complex environment that allows this to happen.

There *is* a more effective way of "organizing" education than the old way inherited from an agricultural age when we thought we could pigeonhole information into human beings. When we designed the old classrooms, we knew much less than we do now about the human lives and brains sitting in chairs. With the knowledge explosion and the vastness of information now available to everyone in the technological age, the old way of organizing education looks ludicrous. It's like keeping people handicapped by keeping on teaching them. It's not education.

Fundamentally, perhaps, there's never been an age in which human life was sacred. Maybe that's still to come.....

Reprinted with permission of *Dromenon, Journal of New Ways of Being.* Volume I, No. 5-6, February, 1979.

APPENDIX II

Workshop Pages

	X FACTOR							**Y FACTOR**					
A.	6	5	4	3	2	1	0	1	2	3	4	5	6
B.	6	5	4	3	2	1	0	1	2	3	4	5	6
C.	6	5	4	3	2	1	0	1	2	3	4	5	6
D.	6	5	4	3	2	1	0	1	2	3	4	5	6
E.	6	5	4	3	2	1	0	1	2	3	4	5	6
F.	6	5	4	3	2	1	0	1	2	3	4	5	6
G.	6	5	4	3	2	1	0	1	2	3	4	5	6
H.	6	5	4	3	2	1	0	1	2	3	4	5	6
I.	6	5	4	3	2	1	0	1	2	3	4	5	6
J.	6	5	4	3	2	1	0	1	2	3	4	5	6
K.	6	5	4	3	2	1	0	1	2	3	4	5	6
L.	6	5	4	3	2	1	0	1	2	3	4	5	6
M.	6	5	4	3	2	1	0	1	2	3	4	5	6
N.	6	5	4	3	2	1	0	1	2	3	4	5	6
O.	6	5	4	3	2	1	0	1	2	3	4	5	6
P.	6	5	4	3	2	1	0	1	2	3	4	5	6
Q.	6	5	4	3	2	1	0	1	2	3	4	5	6
R.	6	5	4	3	2	1	0	1	2	3	4	5	6
S.	6	5	4	3	2	1	0	1	2	3	4	5	6
T.	6	5	4	3	2	1	0	1	2	3	4	5	6

X Factor _____

Y Factor _____

_____

_____

_____

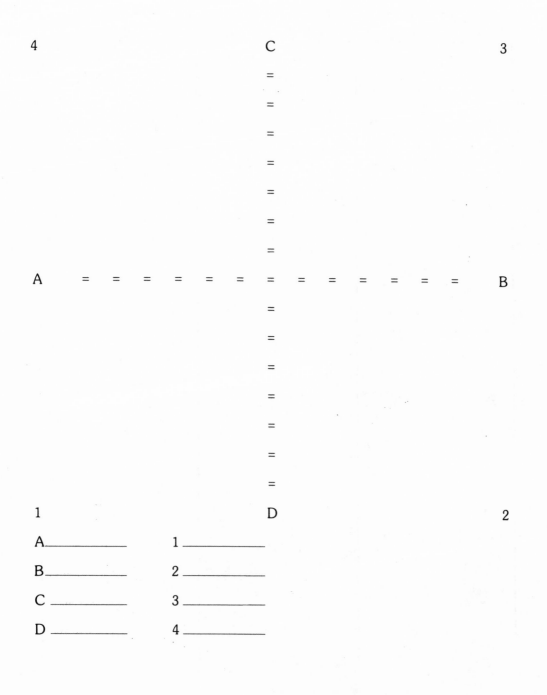

4

C

3

A = = = = = = = = = = = = B

1

D

2

A_____   1_____

B_____   2_____

C _____   3 _____

D _____   4_____

AHA !

OH NO !

Musical Memory

I remember...	clearly	vaguely	not at all
1. the first time I whistled	——	——	——
2. my first opera	——	——	——
3. my first record player	——	——	——
4. my first recital	——	——	——
5. my 4th grade music teacher	——	——	——
6. my favorite song at age 7	——	——	——
7. an action song from age 5	——	——	——
8. dancing at age 6	——	——	——
9. my first piano lesson	——	——	——
10. my first music contest	——	——	——
11. the first time I heard a pipe organ	——	——	——
12. the smell of my first instrument case	——	——	——
13. the food served after a concert	——	——	——
14. the first time I saw a marching band	——	——	——
15. the music played at John F. Kennedy's funeral	——	——	——
16. my most boring music teacher	——	——	——
17. the smell of my music teacher's house	——	——	——
18. the touch and sound of my first piano	——	——	——
19. my favorite record in high school	——	——	——
20. the record jacket of a Christmas present	——	——	——
21. tastes associated with listening to music	——	——	——

WORKSHOP NOTES

WORKSHOP NOTES

WORKSHOP NOTES

WORKSHOP NOTES

WORKSHOP NOTES

WORKSHOP NOTES

WORKSHOP NOTES

BIBLIOGRAPHY
Introduction to the Musical Brain
Don G. Campbell © 1983

Ayres, A. Jean. SENSORY INTEGRATION AND THE CHILD.
Western Psychological Services, Los Angeles, 1979.

Beebe, Robin Van Doren. SKIPPING STONES, REFLECTIONS ON THE
CREATION OF MEANING. Private Printing, Ojai, CA, 1980.

Bennett, Thomas L. BRAIN AND BEHAVIOR.
Wadsworth Publishing Co., Belmont, CA, 1977.

Bever, T.G. and Chiarello, R.L. "Cerebral Dominance in Musicians and Non-Musicians."
SCIENCE, May, 1974.

Bloom, Benjamin. TAXONOMY OF EDUCATIONAL OBJECTIVES. David McKay,
New York, 1956.

Bonny, Helen, and Savary, Louis, MUSIC AND YOUR MIND.
Institute for Consciousness and Music, WA., 1973.

Bono, E. de. CHILDREN SOLVE PROBLEMS.
Harper and Row, New York, 1974.

Buzan, Tony and Dixon, Terence. THE EVOLVING BRAIN.
Holt, Rinehart, and Winston, New York, 1978.

Buzan, Tony. USING BOTH SIDES OF YOUR BRAIN.
E.P. Dutton, New York, 1976.

Chall, J. and Mirsky, A. EDUCATION AND THE BRAIN.
University of Chicago Press, 1978.

Clynes, Manfred. MUSIC, MIND AND BRAIN: THE NEURO-PSYCHOLOGY
OF MUSIC. Plenum Press, New York, 1982.

Critchley, MacDonald and Henson, R.A. MUSIC AND THE BRAIN: STUDIES IN
THE NEUROLOGY OF MUSIC. W. Heinemann Medical Books, London. 1977.

Feder, Elaine and Bernard. THE EXPRESSIVE ARTS THERAPIES.
Prentice-Hall, Englewood Cliffs, N.J. 1981.

Feldenkrais, Moshe. AWARENESS THROUGH MOVEMENT.
Harper and Row, New York, 1971.

Ferguson, Marilyn, ed. BRAIN MIND BULLETIN.
Box 42211, Los Angeles 90042.

Ferguson, Marilyn. THE BRAIN REVOLUTION.
Taplinger, New York, 1973.

Fisher, Richard B. BRAIN GAMES.
Schocken, New York, 1982.

Gardner, Howard. "Do Babies Sing a Universal Song?"
from *Psychology Today*, December, 1981.

Gardner, Howard. THE ARTS AND HUMAN DEVELOPMENT: A
PSYCHOLOGICAL STUDY OF THE ARTISTIC PROCESS. John Wiley and
Sons, New York, 1973.

Gazzaniga, Michael S. and LeDoux, Joseph. THE INTEGRATED MIND.
Plenum Press, New York, 1978.

Goleman, Daniel. "Holographic Memory."
from Psychology Today, February, 1979.

Halpern, Steven. TUNING THE HUMAN INSTRUMENT.
Spectrum Research, Belmont, CA, 1978.

Hamel, Peter Michael. THROUGH MUSIC TO THE SELF.
Shambhala, Boulder, 1978.

Hampden-Turner, Charles, MAPS OF THE MIND.
Collier Books, New York, 1981.

HEMISPHERE LATERALITY AND MUSIC.
Proceedings Report of the Second Annual Loyola Symposium. Loyola University,
New Orleans, 1979.

Henri, Robert. THE ART SPIRIT.
 Lippincott, Philadelphia, 1923.

Hermann, Evelyn. SUZUKI, THE MAN AND HIS PHILOSOPHY.
 Ability Development, Athens, OH, 1981.

Hollander, Lorin. "The Study of the Piano As a Discipline for Self-Understanding and as a Metaphor for the Path of Enlightenment." from Noteworthy Piano News from Kjos, Spring, 1980.

Houston, Jean and Masters, R.E.L. LISTENING TO THE BODY.
 Dell, New York, 1972.

Houston, Jean. THE POSSIBLE HUMAN.
 J.P. Tarcher, Los Angeles, 1982.

Illich, I.D. CELEBRATION OF AWARENESS.
 Calder and Boyars, 1971.

Kenney, Maureen. CIRCLE ROUND THE ZERO.
 Magnamusic Baton, St. Louis, 1975.

Leonard, George. EDUCATION AND ECSTASY.
 Dell, New York, 1968.

Leonard, George, THE SILENT PULSE.
 E.P. Dutton, New York, 1978.

Lilly, John C. THE HUMAN BIOCOMPUTER.
 Julian Press, New York, 1972.

Lozanov, Georgi. SUGGESTOLOGY AND OUTLINES OF SUGGESTOPEDY.
 Gordon and Breach, New York, 1978.

McCarthy, Bernice. THE 4 MAT SYSTEM.
 Excel, Inc., Arlington Heights, IL 1980.

McGee-Cooper, Ann. BUILDING BRAIN POWER.
 McGee-Cooper Enterprises, 4236 Hockaday, Dallas, Texas 75229, 1982.

Murdock, Maureen. SPINNING INWARD.
 Kenzel Publications, 767 Gladys Ave., Long Beach, CA 90804, 1982.

Orff, Carl. THE SCHULWERK. Vol. 3 of DOCUMENTATION: HIS LIFE AND
 WORK. Translated by Margaret Murray. Schott Music Corp, New York, 1978.

Orff, Gertrud. THE ORFF MUSIC THERAPY.
 Schott, London, 1980.

Ornstein, Robert. THE NATURE OF HUMAN CONSCIOUSNESS.
 Freeman, New York, 1973.

Ornstein, Robert. THE PSYCHOLOGY OF CONSCIOUSNESS.
 Freeman, New York, 1972.

Ostrander, Sheila & Schroeder, Lynn. SUPERLEARNING.
 Delta Press, New York, 1979.

Penfield, Wilder. THE MYSTERY OF THE MIND.
 Princeton University Press, Princeton, 1975.

Prettyman, Jane, ed. "Matters of Consequence". Dromenon, Journal of New Ways of
 Being. Vol. I, No 5-6 February, 1979. New York.

Regelski, Thomas A. ART EDUCATION AND BRAIN RESEARCH.
 Menc, Reston, VA., 1978.

Rose, Steven. THE CONSCIOUS BRAIN.
 Vintage Books, New York, 1976.

Rose, Steven and Russell, Peter. THE GLOBAL BRAIN.
 J.T. Tarcher and Co., Los Angeles, 1983.

St. Exupéry, Antoine de. THE LITTLE PRINCE.
 Harcourt, Brace and Jovanovich, New York, 1962.

Samples, Bob. THE METAPHORIC MIND.
 Addison-Wesley, Reading, Mass, 1978.

Samples, Bob. THE WHOLESCHOOL BOOK.
 Addison-Wesley, Reading, Mass, 1978.

Samuels, M. and Samuels, N. SEEING WITH THE MIND'S EYE.
    Random House, New York, 1975.

Schafer, R. Murray. THE TUNING OF THE WORLD.
    Alfred Knopf, New York, 1977.

Silver, Rawley A. DEVELOPING COGNITIVE AND CREATIVE SKILLS
    THROUGH THE ARTS. University Park Press, Baltimore, 1978.

Stebbing, Lionel, ed. MUSIC.
    New Knowledge Books, W. Sussex, England.

Taylor, Gordon R. THE NATURAL HISTORY OF THE MIND.
    E.P. Dutton, New York, 1979.

Timms, Moira. THE SIX-O'CLOCK BUS.
    Turnstone Press, Wellingsborough, England, 1979.

Virshup, Evelyn. RIGHT BRAIN PEOPLE IN A LEFT BRAIN WORLD.
    Guild of Tutors Press, Los Angeles, 1978.

Vitale, Barbara Meister. UNICORNS ARE REAL.
    Jalmar Press, 45 Hitching Post Dr., Rolling Hills Estates, CA 90274, 1982.